THINK
ON
THESE
THINGS

THINK ON THESE THINGS

60 THOUGHTFUL DEVOTIONS FOR RENEWED PEACE

LORI HATCHER

Our Daily Bread
Publishing.

Think on These Things: 60 Thoughtful Devotions for Renewed Peace
© 2025 by Lori Hatcher

Interior design by Michael J. Williams

ISBN,978-1-916718-47-0

Library of Congress Cataloging-in-Publication Data Available

Printed in the United Kingdom
25 26 27 28 29 30 31 32 / 8 7 6 5 4 3 2 1

To God, who created everything true, noble, right, pure, lovely, admirable, excellent, and praiseworthy. Thank You.

Contents

Introduction
An Invitation

When you hear the word *peace*, what comes to mind? Busy toddlers napping, bringing silence to an otherwise noisy home? Or an absence of relational conflict, in your marriage, family, or church? Some might picture peace as the end of a cultural or global war.

Reverend Billy Graham noted, "The word *peace* is used in the Bible in three main ways. First, there is spiritual peace—peace between God and man. Second, there is psychological peace—peace within. Third, there is relational peace—peace among mankind."[1]

Every believer has experienced the first kind of peace—spiritual peace, made possible because of Christ's death on the cross. If we've confessed our sin to God and surrendered our lives to His control, we stand before Him forgiven and free.

We won't fully experience the third type of peace—relational peace among humanity—until Christ, the Prince of Peace, ushers in His eternal kingdom.

But what about the second type, psychological peace? Do you long for it? Wouldn't you love to experience deep, abiding soul rest? Don't you wish you could sleep with nothing troubling your mind? Or laugh from the depths of your soul, unhindered by fear or pain? Do you envy the unbridled joy of a child and long for those carefree days?

Must we wait until Jesus returns and banishes sin and sorrow from our world forever before we experience this kind of soul-satisfying peace?

The Bible tells us we don't have to wait until heaven. We can experience peace right now. Philippians 4:8–9 tells us how: "Finally, brothers and sisters, whatever is true, whatever is noble, whatever is right, whatever is pure, whatever is lovely, whatever is admirable—if anything is excellent or praiseworthy—think about such things. . . . And the God of peace will be with you."

Romans 12:2 calls this being "transformed by the renewing of your mind." Ephesians 4:23 describes it as being "made new in the attitude of your minds."

Scripture assures us that peace is possible when we seize the reins of our mind and point it where we want our thoughts to go. We can "take captive every thought to make it obedient to Christ" (2 Corinthians 10:5).

If you long to experience the peace that will keep your heart joy-filled and secure, I invite you to join me on a sixty-day journey to "think on these things."

You keep him in perfect peace whose mind is stayed on you.

Isaiah 26:3 ESV

~Lori

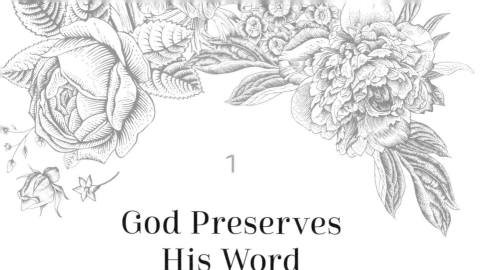

1

God Preserves His Word

As Earl and Cynthia Pierce prepared for bed on Saturday, October 4, 2015, they never suspected what the next few hours would bring. Almost twenty inches of rain had fallen on South Carolina that week, and more was forecast overnight. Meteorologists were calling the weather event the "thousand-year flood,"[2] but Earl wasn't concerned. At worst, he expected to find standing water in his front yard the next day.

Before they turned out the lights, Earl completed his nightly Bible reading, leaving his Bible open on his favorite chair. Cynthia wrote their offering check and set it on the kitchen table.

By 2:30 a.m., their yard was flooded. By 3:30 a.m., water covered the surface of the carport. Before the couple had gathered a change of clothes, Cynthia's purse, and their medication, water was leaking through the baseboards. While Earl turned to lock the door to the house that had been their home for twenty-seven years, Cynthia stepped off the porch—into water that reached her shoulders.

By God's grace, Earl and Cynthia made it out. Neighbors

sent them pictures the next day. Water had risen to eight feet on the outside of their home and five feet inside.

When the waters receded, they returned to find almost everything had been destroyed—with two significant exceptions—Earl's Bible and Cynthia's tithe check. Earl found his Bible, dry and undisturbed, on the chair where he had last read it. Cynthia's check rested on the table, right where she had left it.

"Unlike most of the other furniture submerged in the house, the table and chair had been lifted up by the flood water, suspended, and set down again so gently that neither item was disturbed."[3]

The Pierce's story reminds me of God's promise in Isaiah 40:8: "The grass withers and the flowers fall, but the word of our God endures forever."

We know God doesn't preserve every copy of the Bible. Many have been consumed in fires, buried in earthquakes, and lost in floods. Governments have collected and destroyed copies of the Scriptures as far back as AD 303, when the Roman emperor Diocletian ordered that the Christian Scriptures be confiscated and burned. But God assures us He will preserve His Word forever.

> The grass withers and the flowers fall, but the word of our God endures forever.
>
> Isaiah 40:8

THINK ON THIS

Nothing can destroy God's Word. It will remain forever.

Precious Father, I praise You for the gift of Your Word. I marvel at how You have preserved it for thousands of years. You've kept it safe through wars, uprisings, persecution, and natural disasters. Help me never take the Bible for granted. It is my life, my hope, and my guide.

2

All Is Well

For thirty-two years, I woke up to reveille and went to sleep to taps. I lived in the shadow of one of the largest military training bases in the country, where I'd regularly see tanks, armored personnel carriers, and Humvees driving to and from the base. Soldiers wearing camouflage-colored uniforms attended church with me. The army's presence made me feel safe.

In 2016, my husband and I moved to the suburbs. I missed hearing the morning serenade. Birds, not bugles, accompanied me on my predawn walks.

Last spring, however, a sound louder than bugles or birds echoed through my home. It shook the windows and rattled the doors. My neighbor heard it, too.

"What in the world is that?" I yelled across the front yard.

"F-16s," she called back, shielding her eyes and peering into the sky. "They relocated from the Air National Guard base to the airport in town while they repair the runways."

As if on cue, planes from the 169th Fighter Wing whooshed across the sky, leaving squiggly smoke trails in their wake. I watched the jets until they disappeared. Knowing that the powerful aircraft and the 250 soldiers who attended them resided less than four miles away made me feel protected.

Greater than the feeling I get from living near an army base or a squadron of F-16 fighter jets is the peace and protection I receive from knowing God is my ultimate protector. David the psalmist felt this way, too.

"Whoever dwells in the shelter of the Most High will rest in the shadow of the Almighty," he wrote. "I will say of the LORD, 'He is my refuge and my fortress, my God, in whom I trust'" (Psalm 91:1–2).

With God watching over me, nothing can touch me without His permission. When scary things enter my life, I need not fear. God will either protect me from harm or walk with me through whatever I face. I can trust Him.

As a Girl Scout, I memorized the words to taps: *All is well. Safely rest. God is nigh.*

As a believer, I learned the words of Psalm 91.

Whether I hear the notes or the quote, their truths hold me secure.

> Whoever dwells in the shelter of the Most High will rest in the shadow of the Almighty.
>
> Psalm 91:1

THINK ON THIS

All is well. Safely rest. God is nigh.

Thank You, heavenly Father, that I need not fear the past, the present, or the future because You promise to protect me from anything outside of Your will for me. When scary things touch my life, they, too, are under Your control. You send them to help me, not to harm me. To grow my faith and draw me and others closer to You. Mysterious are Your ways, O Lord, but faithful is Your care over me. Amen.

3

Creation Spotlights Our Creator

I think heaven's going to look a lot like springtime in South Carolina. Where I live, every plant with roots and shoots erupts into bloom, transforming our gray landscape into a pastel paradise. Grass that lay dormant all winter comes alive with a green so bright it shimmers. The air, fresh washed and fragrant, echoes with the sound of baby birds chirping.

Sunshine shrugs off her winter coat and beams like a teenage girl on her way to the prom, dazzling us with her beauty and warming us with her smile. Clouds that once hung heavy now airbrush the sky.

The psalmist never saw a South Carolina spring, but he captured its essence when he penned, "The heavens declare the glory of God; the skies proclaim the work of his hands. Day after day they pour forth speech; night after night they reveal knowledge. They have no speech, they use no words; no sound is heard from them. Yet their voice goes out into all the earth, their words to the ends of the world" (Psalm 19:1–4).

Creation spotlights our Creator, and what a glorious Creator

He is. Paul, perhaps pondering a landscape such as mine, wrote, "For since the creation of the world God's invisible qualities—his eternal power and divine nature—have been clearly seen, being understood from what has been made" (Romans 1:20).

How kind of God to fill our world with evidence of His creativity and complexity. We needn't look far to see hints of His divine attributes—and His compassion. He created sunshine to warm our days. Air to fill our lungs. Growing things to satisfy our hunger for sustenance and for beauty.

I don't know if heaven will look like a South Carolina springtime, but I'm glad I get to enjoy a bit of heaven here on earth. I'm also grateful, whether the landscape outside my window is winter or springtime, gray or green, I don't have to look far to see the beauty of our Creator God.

> The heavens declare the glory of God; the skies proclaim
> the work of his hands.
>
> Psalm 19:1

THINK ON THIS

Creation points to our Creator, and what a glorious Creator He is.

Creator God, You have filled my world with beauty. Everywhere I look, I see Your fingerprints. From the brushstrokes in a sunset to the engineering marvels of an atom, all creation declares Your praise. I lift my eyes

to You, the author of everything, and worship in awe and thanksgiving. Thank You for opening my heart and helping me see You in our world. Amen.

4

Love Gives

"Wait, Gigi!" Caroline called as I reached the door. "I have something for you." She turned and disappeared into her bedroom.

My husband describes Caroline as "no bigger than a squirrel." What she lacks in substance, she makes up for in heart. With one blink of her golden eyes, she can bring a smile to a stressed parent's face, cheer a grumpy friend, or soothe her baby brother. She wails at injustice and champions the marginalized.

She also showers gifts on those she loves. I seldom leave her presence without a treasure in my pocket.

"Here you go, Gigi," she said that day. "It's for you." She dropped a tiny LEGO turtle into my palm and scampered off.

I added the treasure to the collection on my "Caroline shelf." A heart-shaped painted rock, a marble, and a silver key. A tiny vial of pixie dust, a sparkly bead, and a cupcake-shaped eraser. Caroline instinctively knows what most of us take years to learn—love gives.

Centuries ago, Jesus described to Nicodemus the ultimate love gift: "God so loved the world that he gave his one and only Son, that whoever believes in him shall not perish but have eternal life" (John 3:16).

John, the beloved disciple, agreed. "This is how God showed his love among us: He sent his one and only Son into the world that we might live through him" (1 John 4:9).

Ponder this a moment. Don't rush past it. Let the thought of God's extravagant love linger and grow until it fills your heart to bursting. God loved us so much that He gave Jesus. And Jesus loved us so much that He sacrificed His life on a cross to pay for our sin. "Greater love has no one than this: to lay down one's life for one's friends" (John 15:13).

If the love of God fills you, as it does our sweet Caroline, let the overflow splash out onto others. Let us "love because he first loved us" (1 John 4:19).

> God so loved the world that he gave his one and only Son, that whoever believes in him shall not perish but have eternal life.
>
> John 3:16

THINK ON THIS

Ponder this moment. Don't rush past it. God so loved the world that He gave us Jesus.

Father, I don't deserve Your love, and I certainly don't deserve the gift of Jesus. I praise You for Your generous, sacrificial love toward me and toward the world. Thank

You for the people in my life who demonstrate Your love here on earth. Help me be a living expression of Your extravagant love to the people I meet today. In Jesus's name I ask, amen.

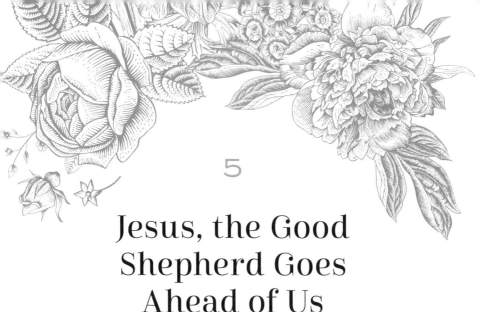

5

Jesus, the Good Shepherd Goes Ahead of Us

Did you know that if a sheep topples over onto its back, it can't right itself? Or that sheep aren't always sweet-smelling, fluffy white wool balls? If their coats get too much lanolin on them, they become sticky and stinky. In 2015, sheep lovers the world over were shocked to hear about a flock of Turkish sheep that launched itself over a cliff following one sheep that decided to end it all.[4]

After reading about the Turkish sheep, I'm comforted that Jesus calls Himself the Good Shepherd (John 10:11). In one of the most comforting verses in the Bible, Jesus gives us a picture of what a good shepherd does: "He calls his own sheep by name and leads them out" (v. 3). The best part of Christ's description of His role as our Good Shepherd tells us, "When he has brought out all his own, he goes on ahead of them" (v. 4).

Did you catch it? "He goes on ahead of them."

Life can be terrifying. Disease. Recession. Divorce. Prodigals. Cultural decay. Political upheaval. Some days I fear what lies ahead. Yet God's Word reminds me that wherever I go and into whatever situation God allows, I'll never go alone.

Jesus will help me navigate the rough spots and guide my feet through uncertain territory. He promises to warn me of danger and feed and sustain me. He'll defend me against my enemies. Unlike the Turkish sheep, we aren't navigating our way unprotected or without a divine guide—we have a Shepherd who will keep us eternally safe and who is always armed. Whatever we face, we can move forward with confidence, knowing that our good, kind, wise, protective warrior Shepherd always goes ahead of us.

> When he has brought out all his own, he goes on ahead of them, and his sheep follow him because they know his voice.
>
> John 10:4

THINK ON THIS

Jesus goes ahead of us into every situation we face.

Jesus, I feel so much comfort and safety when I read how You describe Yourself as the Good Shepherd. I praise You that everything that comes into my life comes from Your good hand. As I walk through the challenges of life, Your willingness to go ahead of me comforts and empowers me. I am never alone with You leading the way.

6

Heaven Smells Like Prayers

My friend Lisa sent a picture of her snowy Ohio backyard. Icicles dripped from the trees. Frost etched lacy patterns on the windows. Like a downy comforter over a chihuahua, a thick blanket of snow obscured everything but the largest objects.

"And aah, the smell," she said. "Nothing like the clean blue smell of snow."

I knew exactly what she meant. Growing up in New England, I delighted in the fragrance of icy air after a snowfall. Cleansed of all toxins, it stings the nostrils with stunning purity.

In heaven, my warmth-loving self hopes I can breathe in the scent of snow without its accompanying cold. Perhaps, because God has washed our sins and cleansed us "whiter than snow" (Psalm 51:7), we'll carry the fragrance of purity with us into heaven.

Have you ever wondered what heaven will smell like? I hope it'll smell like warm chocolate chip cookies. And new babies. And freshly mown grass. Maybe it will have notes of lilac and magnolia. Or the scent of an ocean breeze.

Revelation 5:8 tells us heaven will smell like prayer.

"And when [Jesus] had taken [the scroll], the four living creatures and the twenty-four elders fell down before the Lamb. Each one had a harp and they were holding golden bowls full of incense, which are the prayers of God's people."

When God gave Moses instructions for building the tabernacle, He told him to craft an altar of incense. Morning and evening, a priest would burn the fragrant elements and send the holy scent wafting toward heaven (Exodus 30:1–8). God said that at this place of worship, "I will meet with you" (v. 6).

Today, He meets with us whenever we read His Word and pray. Like the wispy smoke of incense, our prayers ascend to heaven. There, the apostles and the sons of Israel capture them in bowls and raise them before the Lord as a fragrant offering.

Each prayer, offered in faith, rises to God's throne, where He breathes them in and smiles (Revelation 5:8). Surrounded by the glories of heaven, He accepts the worship of our prayers and meets us there.

I look forward to smelling the snow-scented, chocolate-chip-smelling, lilac-magnolia-ocean-breeze-infused air of heaven, but I can't wait to bow before the Lord, who alone is worthy of our prayers.

> Each one had a harp and they were holding golden bowls full of incense, which are the prayers of God's people.
>
> Revelation 5:8

THINK ON THIS

Our prayers, offered in faith, rise to God's throne. Not only does God hear our prayers, He breathes them in as worship.

Father, forgive me for ever doubting that my prayers matter to You. Not only do You hear them; You accept them as a sweet offering of faith and trust. And not only mine, but the prayers of all Your children. How mighty and magnificent You are not only to hear all our prayers, but to work on our behalf. You are a faithful God, worthy of our praise.

7

One Day We'll Frolic with the Animals

I 'm a city girl. Whether the backdrop of my life has been the choppy waters of Narragansett Bay in small-town Rhode Island or the city streets of Columbia, South Carolina, I've always lived in suburbia. This is why I get so excited about anything farmy. Baby chicks, goats, and pigs make me squeal. I want to pet every critter I can get my hands on.

One day, while visiting my friend Maureen's North Carolina farm, I watched the sun sink low in the sky. The cows that had dotted the hillside all day had meandered down toward the barn that flanked her house.

I'd never seen a Highland cow up close, so I sauntered up to the fence. From a distance, the shaggy-haired, big-eyed bovines looked cute enough to pet. Up close, their fearsome horns and massive size made my heart quicken. A flicker of fear quivered in my chest.

If it wasn't for that barbed-wire electrical fence, I realized, that cow could make shish kebab out of me. I stepped back and didn't turn around until I'd put a safe distance between me and the two-ton creature.

The early chapters of Genesis refer to a time in history when humankind and animals interacted in peaceful community. Only after the flood did the element of fear enter into animal/animal and human/animal relationships (Genesis 9:2).

When Christ returns, God will again banish fear between animal species and between animals and humankind. Isaiah 11:6 describes this beautiful scene: "The wolf will live with the lamb, the leopard will lie down with the goat, the calf and the lion and the yearling together; and a little child will lead them."

When I dream of Christ's return, I picture myself cuddling with a cheetah and snuggling a koala. I want to pet elephants, ostriches, and alligators. Snakes won't give me the heebie-jeebies, nor will spiders send me screaming. I might even ride a Highland cow.

Or maybe I won't. Friendly or not, those horns are awfully large.

> The wolf will live with the lamb, the leopard will lie down with the goat, the calf and the lion and the yearling together; and a little child will lead them.
>
> Isaiah 11:6

THINK ON THIS

One day, God will remove our fear, and we'll frolic with the animals.

Jesus, Your creativity leaves me speechless. From the fluffy puppy to the mighty whale, Your power and imagination has filled our world with living creatures. I can't wait for the day when I can interact with the creatures You have made—all of them—without fear or hesitation. What fun that will be!

8

In Heaven, We'll Have Brand-New Bodies

What child doesn't wish they could fly? Or climb walls like Spider-Man? Or swim underwater without ever running out of oxygen?

When I was young, I dreamed of climbing Colorado's Pikes Peak. The highest peak in my home state of Rhode Island is Jerimoth Hill, which rises to an underwhelming height of 810 feet. To me, the 14,110-foot Colorado mountain represented the pinnacle of US mountain climbing. And Gertrude Ederle represented the pinnacle of swimming.

Gertrude was the first woman to swim the 21-mile-long English Channel. She not only swam it but held the world record for 35 years with a time of 14 hours and 39 minutes. Some days, I imagined myself as Gertrude, skimming through the frigid Atlantic waters, dodging sharks and jellyfish.

Sadly, I've accomplished neither of these physical feats. I've also never flown (without an airplane), climbed walls, or swum the depths of the ocean without an oxygen tank. My body is limited and grows even more limited as I age. Maybe this is why I love the description in 1 Corinthians 15 of the new body God promises us after we die.

"The body that is sown is perishable, it is raised imperishable; it is sown in dishonor, it is raised in glory; it is sown in weakness, it is raised in power; it is sown a natural body, it is raised a spiritual body" (vv. 42–44).

My spiritual body won't be affected by the limitations that plague my mortal body. Sickness and disease won't touch me. Nor will headaches, joint pain, or influenza. The cancer that has ravaged so many of my loved ones won't touch my spiritual body. I'll be able to run from one end of the celestial city to the other without stopping to catch my breath. I might even climb Mount Sinai.

My imaginations, I'm sure, fall far short of what we'll experience when we exchange our earthly bodies for a heavenly body. But I can dream. And so can you.

See that mountain over there? I'll race you to the top. On your mark, get set, *go!*

> We will not all sleep, but we will all be changed—in a flash, in the twinkling of an eye, at the last trumpet. For the trumpet will sound, the dead will be raised imperishable, and we will be changed.
>
> 1 Corinthians 15:51–52

THINK ON THIS

We'll live forever in a body that can race up a mountain but will never be touched by sickness, disease, or death.

Thank You, Jesus, for promising us spiritual bodies that will live forever and be able to do amazing things. To think that all the frailties of our earthly bodies will vanish. Oh, my! No pain. No creaky joints or pulled muscles. No sickness, doctors, or medicines. We'll be stronger than we've ever been and able to do things we've never done before. Heaven is going to be incredible.

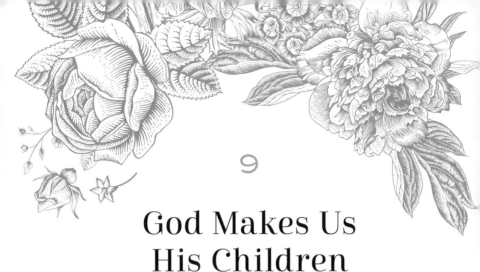

9

God Makes Us His Children

Charles Thomas Hunter III was the long-awaited, recently adopted, third-generation son of so-happy-they-could-sing parents. They couldn't wait to make him part of their family. When Charles Jr. and Abigail signed Charlie's adoption papers, they pledged to love and care for him with every resource they had. And they have—joyously, willingly, lavishly.

When Baby Charlie arrived home from the hospital, you'd have thought one of England's royalty had produced the next heir to the throne. An entourage of cars lined the street for blocks. Enough clothes, toys, and diapers for three babies crowded the nursery. Bottles and a year's supply of formula filled the pantry. A professional photographer and videographer captured every teary smile as his parents ushered him into their home.

First John 3:1 describes another adoptive Parent. "See what great love the Father has lavished on us, that we should be called children of God!" Like Charles and Abigail, our heavenly Father not only took an interest in children the world deemed "unwanted," but sought after them. He wholeheartedly welcomed us into His family.

As Charlie's parents weren't content to provide the bare necessities for their son, neither does our beloved Father limit His provision. He opens His heart and home and calls us *beloved children.* He grants us the right to bear His name.

Charlie's homecoming was a glorious celebration, but an even greater celebration erupts every time someone surrenders their life to God. Jesus gave His disciples a peek at what happened in heaven the day God made us His child. "There will be more rejoicing in heaven over one sinner who repents than over ninety-nine righteous persons who do not need to repent" (Luke 15:7).

Once God adopts us into His family, we're no longer nameless orphans. We're sons and daughters of the King of Kings and Lord of Lords. Lavishly loved and enthusiastically celebrated.

Marvel at this.

> See what great love the Father has lavished on us, that we should be called children of God! And that is what we are!
>
> 1 John 3:1

THINK ON THIS

The God of the universe loves us enough to call us His children.

Oh, Father, how mind-boggling to think that You've chosen to make me Your child. To bear Your name. To be part of Your family. Your love overwhelms me. I was so lost, yet You sought me out, called me to Yourself, and made me Your own. I bow before you in humble gratitude. Help me never forget the precious gift of sonship You've given me. In Jesus's name I pray, amen.

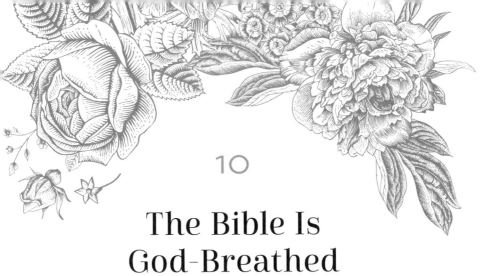

10

The Bible Is
God-Breathed

"DEER MISS CARTER," the note read, "PLEESE EXCUZ TOMMY FROM GYM CLASS TODAY. HE HAS A HURT LEG AND CAN'T RUN."

This wasn't Miss Carter's first note from a "parent." Or her first year in the classroom. She'd been reading notes from parents as far back as chalkboards and mimeograph machines. She could spot counterfeit communication from three desks away, even without her glasses.

Sometimes the paper made her suspicious. Moms didn't usually send notes on composition paper with the fringy edges still attached. Other times, the spelling was off. Or the grammar. Or both. Handwriting was usually a dead giveaway, although once she rejected a note from a third grader only to find out his physician father had indeed written it.

After forty years in the classroom, she assumed parent notes were fake until proven otherwise. Some called her suspicious. Most called her wise. Her motto: Don't believe anything until you confirm it.

I'm grateful even wiser people than Miss Carter confirmed the words we now know as the Bible. In the centuries after Christ's resurrection, church leaders put each book through a rigorous series of tests to confirm its inspiration. That it is "God-breathed" (2 Timothy 3:16). History, archaeology, and external evidence affirm the credibility of God's Word. Logic invites us to see the reliability of the manuscript, but ultimately, we believe by faith that every word "comes from the mouth of the LORD" (Deuteronomy 8:3).

Miss Carter was wise not to trust the words written in a childish scrawl on notebook paper. We are wise to trust the words of the Bible. They come directly from God's mouth, through the quills of men, and into our hearts. We can base our lives—and our eternity on them.

> All Scripture is God-breathed.
>
> 2 Timothy 3:16

THINK ON THIS

We can base our lives—and our eternity—on God's inspired Word.

Thank You, Father, for giving us Your Word. I never have to wish I could hear from You or beg You to reveal Yourself. All I have to do is open the pages of my Bible and drink in Your truth. I praise You for giving me a reliable, trustworthy source of wisdom and insight. I love You so much.

11

We Will Reap the Rewards of Perseverance

From 1970 to 1987, Walter Payton ran more than nine miles. This doesn't sound like much unless you recognize Payton as the veteran running back with the Chicago Bears. And realize that he ran every yard with at least one player trying to tackle or trip him. Over his entire career, he rushed for 16,726 yards and broke the record for most rushing yards by any NFL player in history. This accomplishment secured his spot in the prestigious Pro Football Hall of Fame.

I've never wanted to be an NFL football star, nor do I hope to be inducted to the Pro Football Hall of Fame, but, like Payton, I want to earn rewards for perseverance. He showed how to press on despite obstacles, opposition, and even injury.

God didn't create most of us to dodge enormous men trying to take us down, but He did call us to run the faith race with perseverance. Despite opposition. In the face of insult and injury, He calls us not only to survive, but to rejoice.

James encouraged first-century believers in Jerusalem to

embrace life's trials as a pathway to great blessing. The same is true for us today.

"Consider it pure joy, my brothers and sisters, whenever you face trials of many kinds, because you know that the testing of your faith produces perseverance" (James 1:2–3). Walter Payton had to muscle his way past three-hundred-pound linebackers trying to squash him. We must push through doubt, despair, spiritual opposition, health challenges, financial struggles, and faith crises. But when we persevere, when we cling to the God who holds us, we reap the rewards. "Let perseverance finish its work," James writes, "so that you may be mature and complete, not lacking anything" (v. 4).

As we refuse to allow trials to knock our spiritual feet from under us, we become time-tested witnesses for Christ. In a world darkened by sin, our faith will shine brighter than any NFL trophy, and our lives will testify to God's sustaining grace.

> Consider it pure joy, my brothers and sisters, whenever you face trials of many kinds, because you know that the testing of your faith produces perseverance. Let perseverance finish its work so that you may be mature and complete, not lacking anything.
>
> James 1:2–4

THINK ON THIS

God allows trials in our lives not to harm us but to make us spiritual champions.

Father, only You could use trials for good in my life. I praise You that when the world, the flesh, and the devil throw obstacles in my path, You give me the ability not only to persevere, but to triumph. I embrace the challenges You have allowed into my life with the joy that comes from trusting You. I rejoice that You, the God who loves me, are Lord over all.

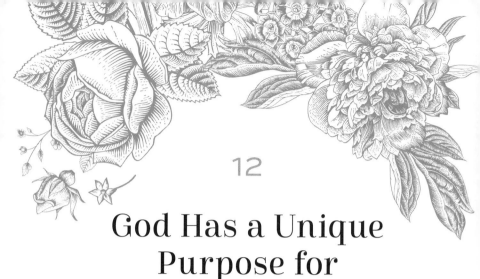

12

God Has a Unique Purpose for Our Design

"I hate having my picture taken," a friend said over lunch. "So do I," another friend chimed in. "I always look frumpy. And my left eye droops."

"Well, at least you have a pretty smile. Mine's lopsided."

The conversation meandered its way from the agonies of adolescent acne, to stretch marks, and finally, to middle-age sags, bags, and crow's feet. Every woman at the table shared at least one aspect of her physical appearance she wished was different.

Our conversation was lighthearted, but I've been part of far more serious conversations. A twelve-year-old asks why his body doesn't produce insulin like other kids'. The parent of an autistic child wonders why their friends' children run and play while hers sits and stares. A five-foot-four teenager looks at his almost six-foot-tall sisters and grapples with why they got the height he wanted.

I suspect Zacchaeus may have wondered the same thing

as he strained to see over the heads of almost everyone in the crowd (Luke 19:3). Moses, who struggled with speech, might have questioned, too (Exodus 4:10).

David, the shepherd/king, may even have been among those who wondered. *Why was I born last of the sons of Jesse? Why do I have ruddy skin?* Yet, instead of despising his birth order or skin color, David took comfort in knowing God had designed him exactly the way He wanted him to be. Not to harm him, but to draw him to Himself.

"For you created my inmost being," he wrote in Psalm 139:13, 15. "You knit me together in my mother's womb. . . . My frame was not hidden from you when I was made in the secret place, when I was woven together in the depths of the earth."

Scripture testifies how Zacchaeus's short stature led him to climb the tree that perfectly positioned him to encounter Jesus. Moses's speech challenges caused him to seek God's enabling, too.

Could it be that God allows our physical bodies, with all their flaws and imperfections, to draw us to Himself? To show us our need to depend on Him? To display His power through our weakness?

Perhaps, instead of lamenting the things we don't like, we should declare with David, "I praise you because I am fearfully and wonderfully made; your works are wonderful, I know that full well" (v. 14).

> For you created my inmost being; you knit me together in my mother's womb.
>
> Psalm 139:13

THINK ON THIS

Our bodies didn't happen by accident. God designed them as they are for His good purposes.

Father, I praise You for Your creative genius in designing my body. You know the purpose You have for my life, and You created my body to accomplish this purpose. Help me trust You to use even my imperfections for good. Whenever I'm tempted to doubt Your purposes, inspire me to praise and thank You instead.

13

God Gives Us Friends

Linda was my first best friend. When we were five, we shared a stoop that joined our tiny apartments. We also shared sleepovers, Barbie dolls, and ice cream from Jimmy the ice cream man. When I spent the night at her house, her mom made Pillsbury cinnamon rolls out of the can, an extravagance our family of five couldn't afford. When she moved away, I cried as if I'd lost my, well, my best friend.

Ellen was my next best friend. She liked to draw as much as I liked to write. One day, her mom told us we could bake chocolate chip cookies. We ate half the raw cookie dough before she got home from work. I didn't eat chocolate chip cookies (raw or baked) for a long time after that.

Linda and Ellen were wonderful friends, but even better than friendships over Barbie dolls and chocolate chip cookies are the friendships I've enjoyed in the family of God.

My sisters in Christ stood in my place when my sister-in-law died suddenly while our family was out of the country on a mission trip. They've prayed me through marital challenges, prodigal children, and health scares. Their faith has challenged me as I've watched them serve God and others.

"Two are better than one," Solomon wrote, "because they have a good return for their labor: If either of them falls down, one can help the other up" (Ecclesiastes 4:9–10).

God knew we'd need godly friends to share wise counsel (Proverbs 27:9), inspire us by their example (Proverbs 27:17), and strengthen us with their companionship (Romans 1:12). Friends make our burdens lighter and our joy deeper.

> There is a friend who sticks closer than a brother.
>
> Proverbs 18:24

THINK ON THIS

God's gift of friendships enhances our lives, ministers to our souls, and enlarges our hearts.

I praise You, Father, for creating our hearts to connect. You placed the Holy Spirit inside every believer, and this Spirit unites us with each other and with You. Thank You for the precious friends You've brought into my life. Help me be the kind of friend that brings joy to another's soul.

14

God Wraps Us in His Embrace

My husband, David, and I were settling in for the night after a busy day of grandparenting. We'd bathed the kids, read them two (more like four) bedtime stories, and fetched each a drink of water, a snack, and another drink of water. Finally, they were asleep. Before we drifted off, we talked about the next day. "If you want to take a walk first thing in the morning," David said, "I'll listen for the kids."

As I tiptoed past the guestroom the next morning, I heard five-year-old Andrew rustling on his bed. *It won't be long before he's up*, I thought. Sure enough, when I returned from my walk, I saw him and David through the living room window. Normally active and animated, Andrew lay quietly with his head on Papa's chest, relishing the comfort of his embrace.

I'm not five years old, but sometimes I imagine what it would be like to crawl up into my heavenly Father's lap and feel His strong arms around me. To rest in the comfort of His embrace. To pour out my heart to Him as He holds me close.

Isaiah understood the tender heart of God and wrote,

"He tends his flock like a shepherd: He gathers the lambs in his arms and carries them close to his heart" (Isaiah 40:11). Although he described God as a mighty warrior (Isaiah 3:2), triumphant King (33:22), and reigning sovereign (6:1), he also included in his book a description of the tender side of God. The perfect Father who loves to gather His children and hold them close.

Some days God the warrior king champions my cause. Other days He wraps me in His arms. I'm grateful He does both.

> He tends his flock like a shepherd: He gathers the lambs
> in his arms and carries them close to his heart.
>
> Isaiah 40:11

THINK ON THIS

God the warrior king is ready to hold you close.

Father, I praise You for always being ready to wrap me in Your arms and hold me. You are both strong and tender, mighty and mild. Thank You for being everything I need. In Jesus's precious name I pray, amen.

15

God Draws Close
When We Pray

Breaking my arm in second grade was the most dramatic event of my early childhood. In a whirlwind of events, I went from lying flat on the ground at the foot of a slide to sitting propped up at home with a plaster cast on my arm.

When Dad and I returned late that evening from the doctor's office, Sandy, my best friend Freddie's mom, stopped by. She brought a treat and a toy to aid my convalescence. My sisters, wide-eyed and more than a little jealous, scrutinized my battle trophy. Mom hugged me, dosed me with baby aspirin, and fed me a much-belated dinner.

She opened the foldout couch, spread a sheet over it, and tucked a few of Granny's crocheted blankets at the foot.

"Dad's going to sleep with you tonight," she said. "In case your arm hurts or you need more medicine." I nodded sleepily.

"Come on, Skate," Dad said, nudging me toward the couch. He tucked a pillow under my arm, settled in beside me, and pulled the covers up.

In the darkness, the pain and fright of the day washed over

me in a tsunami of emotion. I sobbed into my pillow as Dad drew me close.

"Daddy, my arm hurts."

"I know, Baby Girl."

"I was really scared when the doctor pulled on my arm to straighten it out."

"I bet you were. I was a little scared myself."

"Can I ride my bike tomorrow?"

"Not for a while, I'm afraid."

Dad and I didn't sleep much that night, but his presence made the time between darkness and dawn bearable. Every four hours, he handed me two tiny, orange-flavored pills. In between, he fetched water, fluffed my pillow, and comforted me. By morning, the nightmare of the previous day had faded, and my spirit was restored.

I don't know if the Israelites suffered any broken arms during their exodus from Egypt, but I know they faced some awfully scary things. They watched as plagues ravaged the land. On the night of the exodus, they splashed blood on their doorposts and waited for the death angel to pass them by.

Then, before the confetti had settled from their emancipation party, Pharaoh's army came charging up behind them bent on enslaving them once again. Even after the waters of the Red Sea parted to make a way of escape, they still had to battle thirty-six powerful kings on the other side of the sea.

I suspect, in the dark and quiet of their nights, flashbacks of fear and pain raced across their minds and banished their sleep.

All the while, God's presence comforted them. "What other nation is so great as to have their gods near them the way the

Lord our God is near us whenever we pray to him," Moses wrote in Deuteronomy 4:7.

Again and again, they cried out to Him, and God drew near. When they prayed for deliverance, He came to their aid. When they lacked wisdom, He provided it. When they lifted their voices to Him, He heard and answered their prayers.

Unlike the nations who worshiped false gods with wooden faces and unseeing eyes, their God was in the heavens seeing their need, acting on their behalf, and loving them.

> What other nation is so great as to have their gods near them the way the Lord our God is near us whenever we pray to him?
>
> Deuteronomy 4:7

THINK ON THIS

Not every broken part of our life can be mended by a plaster cast and a hug, but great healing is possible when we remember our God is near whenever we pray to Him.

Thank You, Father, for being a living, seeing, tender-hearted God who doesn't run away when my needs become overwhelming. Instead, You draw close and come to my aid. Your presence comforts me, and Your love helps banish my fear. I love You so much.

16

God Has a Heavenly Cure for Insomnia

Have you ever gone to bed and couldn't sleep? Not because of restless leg syndrome, too much caffeine, or indigestion, but because you were worrying? Maybe the circumstances of the day had you on edge. Or concern for a spouse, loved one, or friend niggled at the edges of (or consumed) your mind. Your imagination whirled with frightening what-ifs and sleep vanished faster than warm cookies in a room full of teenagers.

These nights torture us. The more we think, the more anxious we become. Soon we've worked ourselves into a jumbled ball of emotions that banishes sleep forever.

I suspect David, the shepherd king, had more than a few anxious nights. The murderous King Saul chased him all over Israel before David ascended to the throne. The Philistines, Moabites, and a host of other enemies had him in their sights after he became king. If anyone had a reason to lie awake at night worrying, David did.

While I'm sure he lost sleep because of life's challenges, he also discovered a powerful cure for anxiety-induced insomnia—prayer and praise.

"On my bed I remember you," David said to God in Psalm 63:6. "I think of you through the watches of the night." Instead of being consumed by his fears, David directed his thoughts to God. He recounted how majestic and powerful He is (v. 2). How much He loves us (v. 3). How willing He is to come to our aid (v. 7).

As David meditated on God's nature and pondered His faithfulness, his sinking heart soared. He lifted his voice in praise. "Because you are my help, I sing in the shadow of your wings" (v. 7).

I've experienced this type of soul-soaring freedom from insomnia. One night, after torturing myself with worst-case scenarios, I followed David's example. I recited God's qualities: goodness, mercy, power, strength, love, kindness, justice, and grace. I praised Him for being sovereign over the details of my life and the people I love. I declared my trust in Him.

Soon, my panic turned to praise, and the burden of my heart lifted. As grateful tears leaked from my eyes, I rested in peace and fell asleep, wrapped in a blanket of God's love.

I'm grateful God doesn't leave us alone in our fearful insomnia. Instead, He provides a prescription for a great night's sleep.

> On my bed I remember you; I think of you through the watches of the night. Because you are my help, I sing in the shadow of your wings.
>
> Psalm 63:6–7

THINK ON THIS

When we praise instead of panic, our hearts rest secure, and our sleep is sweet.

Father, I will praise You as long as I live. Your love is better than life. You satisfy every need of my heart and fill me with peace and joy in Your presence. May my lips always bring You praise.

17

We Can Forgive as God Does

I never meant to break a confidence. Or hurt my friend Linnea. But I did. I shared information she meant only for me and put her and her family in an awkward situation. Thankfully, Linnea was a mature believer who knew how to handle my indiscretion. She expressed her feelings to me (and me alone) and listened to my perspective. When I apologized and asked her to forgive me, she did. Wholeheartedly.

How do I know?

Because she doesn't remember the incident. At all.

I, on the other hand, have never forgotten it. Or the shame I felt during our dreadful conversation. When I decided to share the story in one of my books, I knew I'd have to ask her permission.

"I don't remember that," she said. Thankfully, she didn't ask me to refresh her memory. Linnea demonstrated one of the amazing characteristics of biblical love—she kept no record of wrongs.

Have you ever been forgiven like this? Forgiven to the point of forgetting? If you're a Christian, you have. Hebrews 10:17 (NLT) tells us, because of Christ's sacrificial death on the cross, "I [God] will never again remember their sins and lawless deeds." Isaiah 43:25 reinforces this truth. "I, even I, am he who blots out your transgressions, for my own sake, and remembers your sins no more."

When we forgive as God does, we act most like Him. And this is a beautiful thing.

> [Love] does not dishonor others, it is not self-seeking, it
> is not easily angered, it keeps no record of wrongs.
>
> 1 Corinthians 13:5

THINK ON THIS

We demonstrate God-like love when we keep no record of wrongs.

Oh, Father, when I think of the sins I've committed that have offended Your holy heart, I hang my head in shame. But when I embrace the forgiveness You extend toward me to cover those sins, I rejoice. Thank You for enabling me to follow Your example and wholeheartedly forgive those who sin against me.

18

Giving Is Better than Receiving

"We're going to buy a goat for Christmas."

When my husband announced this to our youth group, the kids thought he was joking.

"A goat? Why do we need a goat?"

"We don't need a goat," David said, "but there's a family in an impoverished country that does. A goat can provide milk and cheese, and what they don't use, they can sell. A dairy animal can lift a family out of poverty."

He showed the kids the picture in the gift catalog and said, "I want to challenge you, during the next month, to look for ways to earn, save, or sacrifice to donate to the Goat Fund." He looked a few in the eyes and said, "Don't ask your parents for it. I want you to give sacrificially. King David said he'd never sacrifice something that didn't cost him (2 Samuel 24:24), and neither will we."

The apostle Paul similarly challenged the elders of the Ephesian church. "I commit you to God and to the word of his grace" (Acts 20:32). Then He encouraged them to "help the weak" and reminded them of Jesus's words, "It is more blessed to give than to receive" (v. 35).

The financial goal David set for our small youth group was lofty, but the students' enthusiasm grew as the month went on. Each week, they dropped dollar bills into the Goat Fund and shared how they'd earned the money. One girl babysat for her siblings. Another cleaned out a neighbor's garage. One of our poorest students skipped lunch for a week to donate her lunch money. "This was the funnest Christmas gift I've ever bought," she said. The other students agreed. "We should do this every year."

David smiled. I'm sure God did, too.

> In everything I did, I showed you that by this kind of hard work we must help the weak, remembering the words the Lord Jesus himself said: "It is more blessed to give than to receive."
>
> Acts 20:35

THINK ON THIS

The joy we feel when we sacrificially give to those in need far outweighs the temporary pleasure we feel when we receive something for ourselves. And our rewards in heaven last forever.

Thank You, Father, that every good gift comes from above, and the ability to give to others comes from You. Thank

You for calling us to give unselfishly so we can experience the deep and abiding joy of sharing our resources with others. I praise You for transforming our hearts to reflect Yours, for You, Father, are the greatest Giver of all.

19

God Chose Us

Five-year-old Linda[5] didn't remember what it felt like to be loved. Perhaps her mother had loved her—once. But that love hadn't been enough to keep her from abandoning Linda and her three siblings.

Maybe her father had loved her, but whatever love he might have felt toward his children had grown colder than the unheated shack he left them in each morning when he went to work. One thing is for certain. Love doesn't tie your three-year-old daughter's ankle to a table leg or leave her nine-month-old baby sister wrapped in urine-soaked rags in a dresser drawer.

Although Linda remembers what it felt like to be unloved, she also remembers what it feels like to be chosen. To be summoned by the orphanage worker, hastily bathed and dressed, and ushered in to meet a kind-faced man and woman in church clothes.

"We want you to be our daughter," the man said. "To live in our home and be part of our family."

Moses reminded the children of Israel that they were loved—and chosen. "To the LORD your God belong the heavens, even the highest heavens, the earth and everything in it," he said.

"Yet the LORD set his affection on your ancestors and loved them, *and he chose you*, their descendants, above all the nations" (Deuteronomy 10:14–15; emphasis added).

God didn't choose Israel as the nation through which the Messiah would come because of their size—they were one of the smallest nations (Deuteronomy 7:7–9). He didn't choose us as His children because we were wise, influential, or titled (1 Corinthians 1:25).

He chose Israel, and He chose us because of who He is—a merciful and kind Father. Titus 3:5 declares, "He saved us, not because of righteous things we had done, but because of his mercy."

Five-year-old Linda had nothing to offer her adoptive parents, yet they chose her to be their daughter. To protect, provide for, and care for her. To seek her good and love her all the days of their lives.

Like Linda, we have nothing to offer our heavenly Father, yet He chose us anyway. To protect, provide for, and care for us. To seek our good and love us all the days of our lives.

He chose us. He *chose* us. He chose *us*!

Marvel and be amazed.

> Yet the LORD set his affection on your ancestors and loved them, and he chose you, their descendants, above all the nations.
>
> Deuteronomy 10:15

THINK ON THIS

God chose *us* to be His children.

Father, I don't deserve Your love, and I certainly can't earn it. But I am infinitely grateful. You drew me to Yourself, saved me, and promised to care for me all the days of my life. I praise You for Your mercy, grace, and loving-kindness.

20

We Can Rejoice
with the Angels

Our church family had prayed for Steve to surrender his life to Christ for years. His wife, Donna, had prayed for decades. Every Wednesday night during prayer meeting, Donna would ask our church family to pray for Steve's salvation.

He'd visit the church on Christmas and Easter, looking painfully uncomfortable in a too-small jacket and tie. Sometimes he'd pick up his daughter Kate from Awana. He'd listen as she chattered all the way home about the verses she'd memorized and the games she'd played.

One day he shocked us by walking through the back doors of the sanctuary and taking a seat up front. He still looked uncomfortable, but he was smiling. And he should have been. His beloved Kate was starring in the Christmas play.

As the notes of Silent Night reached our ears and bathrobe-clad shepherds clomped their way onto the stage, Kate took her place before the microphone. Cradling her baby doll Jesus, she lisped John 3:16, "For God so loved the world that he gave his one and only Son, that whoever believes in him shall not perish but have eternal life."

Steve had heard the words before, but that night he experienced them in a new way. A holy way. An irresistible way.

And his heart cracked wide open.

When the pastor asked if anyone wanted to surrender their life to Christ, Steve strode down the aisle. Donna wept in her pew. Those who had prayed for Steve wiped away happy tears.

During the glorious celebration that followed, an even greater celebration erupted in heaven. Jesus described what it would look like when a lost sheep came home. "There will be more rejoicing in heaven over one sinner who repents than over ninety-nine righteous persons who do not need to repent (Luke 15:7).

I don't know if celestial confetti littered God's throne room that night, but I could almost hear the joyous shouts echoing off the golden streets and the heavenly trumpets sounding. More than a few saints shouted themselves hoarse as God welcomed another lost son into the family.

> I tell you that in the same way, there will be more rejoicing in heaven over one sinner who repents than over ninety-nine righteous persons who do not need to repent.
>
> Luke 15:7

THINK ON THIS

Heaven erupts in celebration every time someone surrenders their life to Christ.

*Oh, Father, thank You for calling people into a relation-
ship with You and allowing us to share in heaven's joy. I
praise You that You never stop drawing people to Yourself,
even those we fear are too hard-hearted to respond. My
lips praise You, and my heart soars as I imagine what
heaven will look like one day when You call us all home.
Hallelujah!*

21

God Loved Us When We Were Unlovable

For the first eighteen years of my life, I considered myself a pretty good person. By the world's standards, I was. I did well in school, was kind to children and the elderly, and returned my library books on time. I never cheated on an exam, got arrested, or killed someone (although I thought about it a few times).

But if you spent any time with me, you soon discovered I was selfish, self-centered, and lazy. Like Dr. Seuss's Grinch, my heart was full of unwashed socks, and my soul was full of gunk.

One day, in a moment I compare to a less-dramatic version of the apostle Paul's epiphany on the Damascus Road (Acts 9), God stripped away my self-righteousness and revealed to me my true nature. I saw, as Isaiah described, that my "righteous acts" amounted to no more than filthy rags compared to God's standard of perfection (Isaiah 64:6). I was spiritually bankrupt.

But the good news, the glorious news, is that "while we were still sinners, Christ died for us" (Romans 5:8). He didn't wait for us to clean up our act, do better, or try harder. He died for us *while* we had our backs turned toward Him and gloried in our sin. When pleasing Him was the furthest thing from our minds.

Jesus stretched out His holy arms, bowed His bleeding head, and died in our place. The just for the unjust. The perfect for the imperfect. The holy for the hopeless.

Savor this. Marvel at the thought that God loved us so much that He sacrificed His only Son to pay our sin debt and make a way for us to have a relationship with Him.

All while we were still sinners.

> But God demonstrates his own love for us in this: While we were still sinners, Christ died for us.
>
> Romans 5:8

THINK ON THIS

Jesus didn't wait for us to become lovable. He loved us in spite of ourselves.

Father, I don't deserve Your love. Jesus, I don't deserve Your sacrifice. You knew this, yet You loved me anyway. Long before You drew me to Yourself, You prepared a way for me to come to You. My heart soars in praise at the magnitude of Your grace-filled gift. I love You so much, God. Help me love You more.

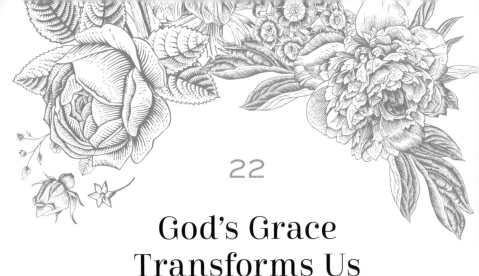

22

God's Grace Transforms Us

W hen I came to faith in Christ, I knew my behavior was supposed to change. I just didn't know how to make it happen. Was I supposed to wake up each morning determined to be good? Or make a solemn vow not to lose my temper, gossip, or speed? Should I draw up a checklist of the most common sins and schedule periodic evaluations with myself to check my progress? How did sanctification (becoming more like Jesus) work?

While I pondered these questions, unbeknownst to me, something inside me was already changing. A force, which I later learned was called *grace*, had begun its work. The same force that had saved me was now making me into a disciple of Jesus.

"It [grace] teaches us to say 'No' to ungodliness and worldly passions, and to live self-controlled, upright and godly lives in this present age" (Titus 2:11–12). From the inside out, grace transforms us.

God's grace, not our self-determination or iron will, provides both the desire and the power to change. As Titus so eloquently wrote, Christ died "to redeem us from all wickedness and to purify for himself a people that are his very own, eager to do what is good" (v. 14).

When I cooperated with grace's gentle (and not-so-gentle) urgings, I made better choices and exchanged poor habits for godly ones. When I fought or ignored the prompting in my spirit, my progress stalled. Choice by choice, God gave me the power to become more like my Savior.

I'm so grateful that after God saves us, He doesn't turn us loose to navigate the rest of our Christian lives in our own strength. As the words of the beloved hymn declare, "'Tis grace has brought me safe thus far, and grace will lead me home."[6]

> For the grace of God has appeared that offers salvation to all people. It teaches us to say "No" to ungodliness and worldly passions, and to live self-controlled, upright and godly lives in this present age.
>
> Titus 2:11–12

THINK ON THIS

God's grace provides the power we need to honor God with our lives.

Grace, grace, God's grace. Grace that exceeds our sin and our guilt.[7] Oh, Father, how kind You are to lavish Your grace upon us. First You save us. Then You give us the ability to say no to what will harm us and yes to what

will bless us. I praise You, Father, Son, and Holy Spirit for the good work You have done and continue to do in me. May I glorify You today with all I say and do. In Jesus's precious name I pray, amen.

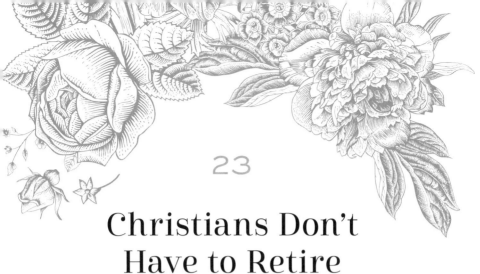

23

Christians Don't Have to Retire

"I had a birthday last week," Ms. Mattie said. "A big one."

"Are you officially a senior citizen now?" I said with a smile.

She threw her head back and cackled, knocking her wig slightly askew. She centered it, smoothed a wayward strand from her forehead, then waved her hand dismissively. "Senior citizens are babies. I'm ninety years old."

Ms. Mattie's driver takes her to the grocery store, to the beauty shop, and to church, where she sings in the choir and crochets baby blankets for the crisis pregnancy center. Every morning she prays through a list of requests longer than my grocery receipt. When testimony time comes around, she's always the first to declare, "God's been so good to me. I love Him more every day."

I taught the women's Bible study Ms. Mattie attended. Knowing she'd be sitting on the front row listening carefully made me study extra hard. Not only did she know how to crochet; she knew her Bible.

Ms. Mattie's lifelong love for God reminds me of the prophet

Daniel. Snatched from his family as a teenager and exiled to Babylon with other Israelite captives, he was forced to serve the wicked king Nebuchadnezzar.

His captors soon recognized his wisdom, and despite his young age and ethnicity, he rose to prominence in the government. He served three pagan kings for more than seventy years.

Like Ms. Mattie, Daniel knew he needed God's power to remain faithful to the Lord in the pagan culture in which he lived. He prayed three times a day toward Jerusalem. He studied God's Word. He spoke the truth and stood for right, even at the risk of becoming a lion's lunch.

Senior saints like Ms. Mattie and Daniel model how to fight the good fight, finish the race, and keep the faith. With God's help, we, too, can love and serve God to the end of our lives. Imagine the joy we'll feel when we stand before Christ to receive "the crown of righteousness, which the Lord, the righteous Judge, will award" (2 Timothy 4:8).

> And Daniel remained there until the first year of King Cyrus.
>
> Daniel 1:21

THINK ON THIS

Christians never retire from God's service. With His help, we can serve Him all the days of our lives.

Thank You, Father, for giving us Your Spirit, Your Word, and Your power to enable us to stay true to You all the days of our lives. Even if circumstances make it hard or the culture opposes our faith, we can faithfully follow Christ as long as we live.

24

We Can Glorify God Even in Death

My friend Cayce and I had a frank conversation. She was facing serious health concerns, and several of her symptoms pointed to cancer. "I'm so afraid," she said. "If I die, I know I'll be with Jesus." She lifted her eyes and blinked back the tears that threatened to fall. "But I look at my children . . . they're so young . . . they still need me."

More than anything, I wanted to tell her everything would be fine. The tests would be negative, the doctor would prescribe a medication or surgery, and she'd live a long and happy life. But I couldn't.

I knew, and she did, too, that young mothers get cancer. And sometimes they die. God doesn't fix everything in this life. Sometimes He walks with us through trials instead of rescuing us out of them. If I denied this possibility, we both knew I'd be lying.

I took a deep breath and prayed for the right words. "Cayce, I'm going to pray your tests come back negative. I hope your doctors find out what's causing your problems and prescribe something to cure you. But if it is cancer, God can use your sickness to bring about something good" (Romans 8:28).

Jesus had a similar conversation with the apostle Peter shortly after Jesus's resurrection. "When you are old you will stretch out your hands, and someone else will dress you and lead you where you do not want to go" (John 21:18). John, writing under the inspiration of the Holy Spirit, explained Jesus's words. "Jesus said this to indicate the kind of death by which Peter would glorify God" (v. 19).

Did you catch that? "To indicate the kind of death *by which Peter would glorify God*" (emphasis added).

"God may glorify himself by healing you," I told Cayce. "And I pray He does. But He may allow you to walk through the trial of cancer to grow your faith and draw others to Himself. Either way, if you trust Him, you can glorify God."

"I want to so much," she whispered, clasping and unclasping her hands. "Please pray that I'll trust and follow Him—no matter what."

I placed my hands over her trembling ones and prayed. "God, You know what's best. Be glorified in and through Cayce. Strengthen her faith and help her trust You. In the strong name of Jesus I ask, amen."

> Jesus said this to indicate the kind of death by which Peter would glorify God. Then he said to him, "Follow me!"
>
> John 21:19

THINK ON THIS

God can use even death for our good and His glory when we trust and follow Him.

Father, I praise You that You can use even sickness and death to glorify Yourself. When I commit to trust You—in the good times and in the bad—You'll use my witness to draw others to Yourself. I praise You that our spirits can grow stronger even as our bodies grow weaker. Whether You grant me a long, healthy life or one plagued by illness, I commit to live by faith so I might glorify You.

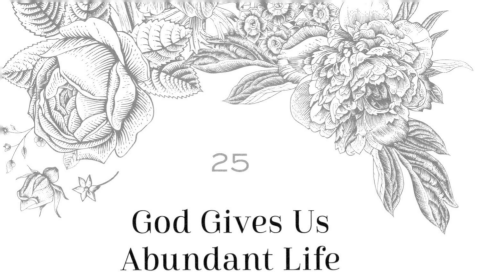

25

God Gives Us Abundant Life

Ashley was thinking hard about Christianity. When a new Christian in our Bible study talked about how good it felt to know God had forgiven his sins, a yearning look came into her eyes. She leaned in when others shared how God had answered a prayer or met a need. One night, a woman who'd recently lost her adult son to cancer described how tenderly God had comforted her in her grief. A tear shimmered in the corner of Ashley's eye.

She lingered after the study. "I'd like to become a Christian," she said. "But I'm afraid I'd have to give up a lot."

I turned to face her. "When I surrendered my life to Christ, I knew there were things in my life that weren't good. Relationships, habits, activities. When I confessed them to God, He removed some immediately, like a relationship that didn't honor Him. Other things slipped away gradually. As I read my Bible and learned more about God, He changed my desires. Instead of forcing me to give up things I loved, He changed my desires so I loved the things He loved."

Ashley nodded.

"But the coolest thing of all," I said, "is how He replaced the bad stuff with so much good that I didn't really miss it. He gave me peace, joy, love, purpose, direction, and comfort. He put me in a family of believers who loves me. My relationship with Him became as real and personal as the friendship I have with you.

"When I asked Christ to be my Savior," I said, "I exchanged my old life for a new one that was filled with joy. Jesus calls it *abundant life*. It has nothing to do with money or possessions and everything to do with a God-filled life."

I paused, and when she lifted her eyes to meet mine, I asked softly, "Wouldn't you like to have a God-filled life?"

"I would," she said, smiling a wobbly smile as one tear slipped down her cheek. "I really would."

> The thief comes only to steal and kill and destroy. I came that they may have life and have it abundantly.
>
> John 10:10 ESV

THINK ON THIS

Abundant life in Christ eclipses any other life.

Why, Father, did I ever wonder if a life following You would be worth it? You have filled my life with a deep, abiding joy that can't compare with anything this world can offer. Thank You.

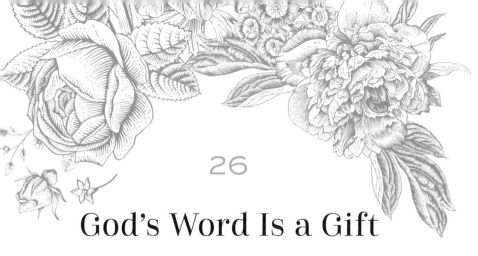

26

God's Word Is a Gift

When I was six, two kind-faced ladies from the Greystone Primitive Methodist church knocked on our door and presented me with a shiny, black King James Version with gold-edged pages. It sat on my shelf, unread, for more than a decade. Then, I surrendered my life to Christ and discovered what a treasure a Bible is.

More miraculous than the physical book, however, is the fact that through the Bible, God speaks His words to humanity. Think about this. The *words* of God. The words of *God*. *The words of God.*

These words have been God-inspired, God-directed, and God-preserved for thousands of years. Inerrant. Infallible. Without contradiction in the original languages. Page after page of hope, truth, and wisdom. And woven throughout the words that span time and history, we find the scarlet thread of God's plan of redemption—from Genesis to Revelation.

Do we need hope? It's there. Direction? In abundance. Wisdom? Read the Proverbs. Inspiration? Delve into the Psalms. Wondering how to live an abundant life now and go to heaven when we die? Spend time in the Gospels and hear from Jesus Himself.

For millennia, God's people had only bits and pieces of God's Word. Parchment scrolls, papyrus sheaves—and two stone tablets inscribed by God. But now, wonder of wonders, we have every word God intended bound between two covers or on an electronic file in our phone or computer. We can hold in our hands a supernatural glimpse into the mind, heart, and purposes of God.

As we marvel at the life-giving words God has given us, may we never neglect or take for granted the precious gift of God's Word.

> For everything that was written in the past was written to teach us, so that through the endurance taught in the Scriptures and the encouragement they provide we might have hope.
>
> Romans 15:4

THINK ON THIS

We can hold in our hands the Word of God.

Father, I praise You for giving us the Bible. Where else will we find hope, help, truth, instruction, comfort, and, best of all, the path to salvation? You didn't have to reveal Yourself to us—You are God and we are not—yet You chose to show Yourself on the pages of

Your Word. Thank You for granting us the privilege of living in an era when we can read the Bible in its entirety. What a gift.

27

God Always Forgives

We intended to go to Chelsea's birthday party. We really did. I bought a gift we knew she'd love. We made a note on the calendar and circled it in red. We even confirmed that we'd be there when we saw Chelsea and her mom, Janine, at the park where our preschool-age girls loved to play.

The invitation had come as a surprise. We didn't move in the same social circles as Janine and her family. Despite our differences, our daughters had become fast friends. While they played, Janine and I got to know each other. When she included us in Chelsea's birthday celebration, I knew it was an important next step in our friendship.

Until I totally and completely forgot about the party. I didn't remember it until three days later when I glanced at Chelsea's gift, wrapped and ready, sitting on the counter.

I called Janine to offer the most sincere apology I knew how to make, but things were never the same. Because I'd made a fatal error, the door to our friendship slammed shut.

I like to think that time, humility, and a few more afternoons at the park might have restored our relationship. Unfortunately, her family moved away before this could happen.

If you've ever been the object of unforgiveness, you know the hurt and frustration it causes. Nothing you do seems to erase the *guilty* stamp on your forehead or to restore your relationship to its preconflict days.

Thankfully, God doesn't treat us like this. The Bible describes Him as one "who blots out your transgressions for my own sake, and I will not remember your sins" (Isaiah 43:25 ESV). When we come to Him with a humble heart, broken and contrite over our sins, He erases our guilt and throws a blanket of forgiveness over our sins. He doesn't hold a grudge, keep a list, or punish us with silence. He wraps us in His love and chooses to forgive.

> You, LORD, are forgiving and good, abounding in love to all who call to you.
>
> Psalm 86:5

THINK ON THIS

God never withholds forgiveness from His children. He always forgives.

Oh, Father, Your heart is so different from mine. So often I want to bear a grudge or withhold forgiveness for the slightest offense. Although You have every right to condemn me for my sins, You choose instead to forgive—every time. I'm so grateful for Your abounding love and undeserved forgiveness.

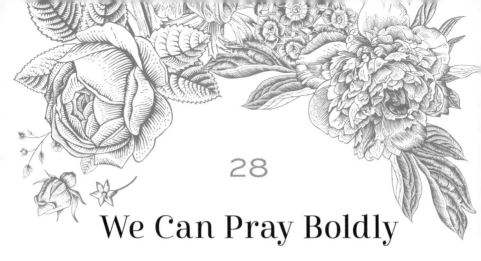

28

We Can Pray Boldly

My grandchildren never hesitate to come to me with their needs.

"Gigi, I'm hungry," one will say, usually five times in any given hour, "Can I have something to eat?"

"Gigi, I was climbing the tree, and my shoe got stuck in the branch. Can you get it out?"

"Gigi, I flushed the toilet, and water's spilling all over the floor. Can you help?"

"Gigi, I'm scared. Will you hold me?"

My grands know I'll help them with every bit of strength and resources I possess. They can bring their needs (and their wants) to me without hesitation. They're not afraid I'll reject them. While I don't always say yes to every request, I'm always willing to listen and do what's best for them. (Except for that day we ate Krispy Kreme doughnuts instead of lunch. The *HOT NOW* sign was on, and even well-intentioned grandmas have an occasional lapse in judgment.)

Unlike my grandkids, I've never felt comfortable asking for help. Sometimes pride makes me hesitate to share a need or make a request. Other times, my reluctance stems from fear.

Will the person say yes or dismiss my request? Or will they laugh and marvel at my presumption? *What makes you think I'd want to help you?*

I used to feel this way about God. Why would the Maker of the universe care about my piddly problems? What right do I have to ask Him for help, especially if my actions caused or contributed to the crisis? I fall far short of His standards. Why should I expect Him to grant my request?

Then one day, I read Hebrews 4:16, and my attitude toward prayer changed faster than the turn arrow in a busy intersection. Because I have a relationship with God, I can come boldly before Him in prayer. I never have to fear He'll mock, scorn, or dismiss my cries for help. I can pour out my heart to Him and trust that He'll do what's right. Every time.

Now, instead of hesitating, trying to earn His favor, or limiting my requests to only "big" things, I approach Him boldly every day—every moment—with the faith and confidence of a beloved child.

> Let us then approach God's throne of grace with confidence, so that we may receive mercy and find grace to help us in our time of need.
>
> Hebrews 4:16

THINK ON THIS

We can approach God boldly with more confidence than a beloved grandchild.

Father, You are mighty, and I am not. You are the glorious God of creation, worthy of glory, honor, and praise. I am needy, troubled, and weak. You know my neediness, yet You make available to me the riches of Your kindness. I can come boldly before You and know You'll never turn me away. I don't deserve Your kindness, but I am infinitely grateful.

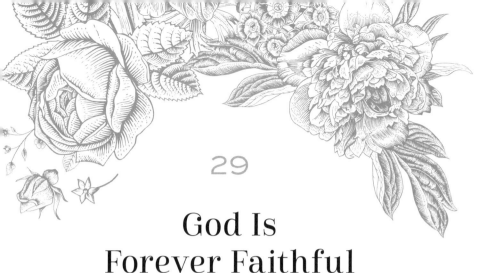

29

God Is
Forever Faithful

My husband, David, and I met Elmer Thompson when he was eighty-eight years old. His kids had decided it wasn't safe for him to drive anymore and asked members of our church to transport him to and from church. We volunteered to drive on Wednesday nights.

Wednesdays soon became our favorite night of the week—not only because of the dynamic Bible study and prayer time, but because of the conversations we had with Mr. Thompson. In the ten-minute drive from his house to the church, he somehow always left a spiritual gold nugget behind.

"What was the highlight of your week?" we asked Mr. T. one Wednesday.

"I had a wonderful talk with my neighbor," he said, "and I had the chance to share the gospel with him." His commitment to tell the good news of Jesus challenged us to share our faith more intentionally.

"What has the Lord taught you this week, Mr. Thompson?" we asked another night.

Think on These Things

"I read in my devotions how mighty God is," he said, "and I just had to lift my hands in worship." His daily habit of reading and responding to God's Word set a profound example for a young couple who was often "too busy" to read our Bibles.

I learned a most powerful lesson the week of his birthday. "I am ninety years old," he said, "and God has cared for me all the days of my life." His eyes filled with tears, and mine did, too. "I am very grateful."

I'd been a Christian for a decade, and I'd experienced God's care and provision. But sometimes I wondered, *Could God—would God—care for me all the way through my life?*

Mr. Thompson's words, backed by his ninety-year testimony, settled the matter in my heart. If I lived for God, He would provide for me.

I'm halfway between thirty and ninety now, and for more than forty years, God has been faithful. Like Mr. Thompson, I often remind young believers how God promises to care for us all the days of our lives. I share stories of how He's met my needs and guided my steps. And I always end our conversation with, "and I am very grateful."

> The LORD your God has blessed you in all the work of your hands. He knows your going through this great wilderness. These forty years the LORD your God has been with you. You have lacked nothing.
>
> Deuteronomy 2:7 ESV

THINK ON THIS

Whether we live to be thirty or ninety, God promises to meet our needs all the days of our lives.

Oh, Father, great is Your faithfulness! From my first breath (and even before) to my last, You have cared for us. You've fed, clothed, and sheltered me. You've met my needs and beyond. Your faithfulness reaches to the heavens. Your love is a vast ocean. I'm very grateful.

30

God Sets Us Apart
for His Purposes

On the top shelf of my kitchen cupboard, a bright yellow plate sits, awaiting its next assignment. My daughter and I painted the masterpiece at a local ceramic shop when she was eight years old. Block letters declare its purpose: CELEBRATE. Cheerful polka dots add to the plate's festive look. The words of Psalm 118:24 (ESV) circle the rim: "This is the day that the LORD has made; let us rejoice and be glad in it."

Our family's celebration plate has helped us commemorate birthdays, anniversaries, graduations, and other joyous occasions. Whether it holds a ribeye steak and a baked potato or a mound of cake and ice cream, its presence declares that the day—and the recipient—is special.

We wouldn't dream of using this beloved piece of pottery for a midweek dinner or a Saturday morning breakfast. We've set it apart, consecrated it for one purpose—to honor someone we love.

Psalm 4:3 (ESV) declares, "But know that the LORD has set apart the godly for himself." As our family has done with our celebration plate, God has set apart His children for one purpose: to celebrate Him.

With this holy calling in mind, everything we do, whether we're raising children, working a job, or caring for a sick loved one, should celebrate the God who redeemed us. Being set apart by a holy God for His glorious purposes gives our life meaning and directs our days. The actions we take, the words we say, and the thoughts we think should honor and glorify Him.

On ordinary days filled with ordinary tasks, Psalm 4:3 reminds us that, in God's eyes, nothing is ordinary. The God of the universe has called us to Himself, set us apart for His purposes, and allows us to have a role in His kingdom work.

This is something worth celebrating.

> But know that the LORD has set apart the godly for himself.
>
> Psalm 4:3 ESV

THINK ON THIS

God has set apart His children for one use—to celebrate Him.

Father, when I think of how You set me apart for a special purpose, my heart takes courage. My life isn't meaningless or random. And when I think about what this purpose is—to celebrate You to the world, oh, my! This calling

is lofty and noble. Only You can fulfill this purpose through me. Be glorified in me, precious Savior, today and every day.

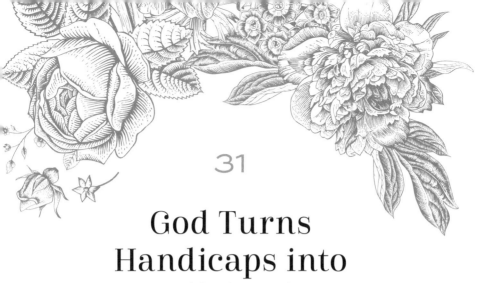

31

God Turns Handicaps into Hallelujahs

Paige is a dark-haired woman with a vibrant smile. She suffers from a disease that has rendered her profoundly deaf and legally blind, confined her to a wheelchair, and made her dependent upon a respirator for every breath.

Paige's disability makes the congenital blindness of the man in John 9 seem trivial. Yet in first-century Israel, to be born blind was to forsake forever the hope of a normal life. The man likely was begging outside the synagogue when Jesus found him.

Jesus's disciples, assuming such a profound disability surely must be God's judgment, asked Him, "Who sinned, this man or his parents, that he was born blind?" (John 9:2).

Jesus's response shocked them all. "Neither this man nor his parents sinned, . . . but this happened *so that the works of God might be displayed in him*" (v. 3; emphasis added).

Christ's answer destroyed the assumption that suffering only comes as a consequence of sin. It also dared to suggest that God had not only allowed the blind man's disability, He orchestrated it.

95

His blindness wasn't a sad twist of fate or the cruel act of a cold-hearted God. It was designed by a loving God to be the velvet backdrop on which to display His sparkling grace, mercy, and power.

Disability advocate Joni Eareckson Tada said, "God deliberately chooses weak, suffering, and unlikely candidates to get His work done, so that in the end, the glory goes to God and not to the person."[8]

Paige admits to asking God questions, but at the age of seventeen, she surrendered her life to Christ. "I knew God had chosen me for His purpose. I really wanted to serve God."

And serve Him she does. With the help of a nurse and an art teacher, Paige has written and illustrated two children's books spotlighting the hope, joy, and unique purpose she embraces. She advocates for people with disabilities, encourages audiences to chase their dreams, and inspires others to see themselves as God sees them.

Centuries ago, Jesus displayed His power and affirmed His deity by healing the blind man. Paige knows her ultimate healing may not come until she meets God in eternity. Nevertheless, she's determined to make the most of every day God gives her. "I want to spend my time on earth serving the Lord as long as I live," she said. Like the blind man, she points others to Jesus and testifies of the great work He has done in her life.

> "Neither this man nor his parents sinned," said Jesus, "but this happened so that the works of God might be displayed in him."
>
> John 9:3

THINK ON THIS

Our disabilities can showcase God's grace, mercy, and power.

Father, only You can take the broken things of this world and make them powerful tools to build Your kingdom. When I surrender my idea of what life should look like and trust Your infinite wisdom, I can see how You use even the sad and bad things for Your glory. I praise You for bringing beauty from ashes when we trust You. What this world calls a handicap, You call a hallelujah.

32

We'll Still Bear Fruit in Our Old Age

On January 9, 2022, Tom Brady became the oldest starting quarterback in NFL history to win a game. He was forty-four years and thirty-seven days old. He added this accomplishment to a long list of "old man" records. Here's a sampling:

- Oldest quarterback to lead the league in passing yards: 5,316 (age forty)
- Most yards in a single season for a quarterback aged forty and older: 5,316 (age forty)
- Oldest player to win NFL MVP: age forty
- Oldest quarterback to win a Super Bowl: age forty years, six months, and five days[9]

Whether you love Tom Brady or hate him, you can't help but admire his NFL accomplishments. He's won the most Super Bowls of any other quarterback with seven wins and only three losses. And, if you're over forty like I am, don't you just love the way he continued to perform, despite his "advanced age"? He made three Super Bowl appearances after he turned forty. Take that, you young whippersnappers!

But what if you can't throw 710 touchdown passes[10] (as of this writing)? What if you're so old you struggle to throw the laundry from the washing machine to the dryer? What hope do you have that your life will have significance, even as your body weakens, sickens, and ages?

What if you're not a Tom Brady?

Psalm 92:12–15 comforts me. It also casts a vision for the rest of my life: "The righteous will flourish like a palm tree, they will grow like a cedar of Lebanon; planted in the house of the LORD, they will flourish in the courts of our God. They will still bear fruit in old age, they will stay fresh and green, proclaiming, 'The LORD is upright; he is my Rock, and there is no wickedness in him.'"

To the end of my life, God's Word assures me, I'll continue to bear fruit. Not necessarily the fruit I bore in my twenties and thirties, but significant fruit. What's the key? Verses fourteen and fifteen tell us. "They will still bear fruit in old age, they will stay fresh and green, proclaiming, 'The LORD is upright; he is my Rock, and there is no wickedness in him.'"

As long as we continue to proclaim, with our words and with our life, that the Lord is upright (present an accurate view of God to others), that He is our Rock (build our lives on Him), and there is no wickedness in Him (trust His actions and His motives), we'll bear fruit in our old age.

Do you want to flourish like a palm tree, grow like a cedar of Lebanon, and bear fruit in your old age? Base your life on

His character and His Word. Trust Him to do His work in and through you. Then tell others about Him.

We may not win an MVP award like Tom Brady, but we can set our eyes on an even greater accomplishment—an MFL award. In God's kingdom, a Most Fruitful Life award trumps MVP every time.

> They will still bear fruit in old age.
>
> Psalm 92:14

THINK ON THIS

Even as we age, we can enjoy a most fruitful life.

Father, I praise You with the words of Psalm 73:26: My flesh and my heart may fail, but You are the strength of my heart and my portion forever. As I age, sometimes I grow discouraged by the things I can't do and the ways I can no longer serve You. I praise You for the promise of Psalm 92:14 that reminds me that even as my body declines, my spiritual fruitfulness doesn't have to. I can still influence others through my words, actions, and prayers. For as long as You grant me life, I pledge to love You and serve You. Be glorified through me today and every day. Amen.

33

Love Banishes Fear

Some people are naturally fearless. Others tremble at a flock of butterflies. Some view life as a challenge to be conquered. Others see it as a threat to be guarded against. Regardless of our disposition, fear eventually comes to all of us. A cancer scare. An adult child determined to self-destruct. A financial crisis.

Big threats produce big fear. Will my husband leave me? Will I survive this treatment? Will I have enough money to retire?

We can't prevent all fear from rising in our hearts. It's a natural response to a real or imagined threat. But we can control what we do with it. If we allow fear to control us, it robs the sleep from our nights and the joy from our days. It affects our prayers, our witness, and our blood pressure. We can't soar in faith when we're cowering in fear.

In a broken world surrounded by sinful people, God knew we'd need an antidote to fear. He revealed it in 1 John 4:18. "There is no fear in love. But perfect love drives out fear."

What kind of love is so perfect it has the power to drive out fear?

Certainly not our love for God—or for others. Our love is weak. Only God's love is strong enough to banish fear from our hearts and replace it with trust. And if we ever doubt His love, we need only look to the cross. "This is how God showed his love among us: He sent his one and only Son into the world that we might live through him" (v. 9).

My friend Jessy and I were texting about her upcoming medical tests. "Please pray for me. I'm so scared." As the day approached, her texts became more frequent and increasingly fearful. I prayed for her, and with her, and shared promises from the Bible. Nothing seemed to help.

On the night before her procedure, however, she sent one last text. "I'm not afraid anymore. I decided it all comes down to this question: Do I trust God? If the answer is yes, then whatever this test reveals, it will be His will for me. In sickness or in health, I can trust Him."

Well said, Jessy. Well said.

> There is no fear in love. But perfect love drives out fear.
>
> 1 John 4:18

THINK ON THIS

When I trust God's perfect love, His love banishes my fears.

God, I don't always understand Your ways, but I know I can trust You. Because You are good, You'll use everything that enters my life for my good, the good of others, and Your glory. Each time I trust You with something scary, You reveal Yourself to me in marvelous ways. Sometimes

You rescue me and fix everything that's broken. Other times, You give me the strength to walk through the trial with my eyes on You. I'm grateful I don't have to be a prisoner to fear. Instead, I can rest in Your love for me. No matter what, I will trust You.

34

God's Word Cheers Our Souls

My friend Linnea and I sat across the table enjoying lunch. Although four states and eight hundred miles separate us, we visit whenever we can. Our times together always end with one or the other asking, "How may I pray for you?"

That day, we talked about health concerns, family challenges, and church struggles. We lamented our culture's moral decline and wondered what the future held for our grandchildren. As we groaned under life's burdens, we remembered the words of Jeremiah the prophet. "The steadfast love of the LORD never ceases; his mercies never come to an end; they are new every morning; great is your faithfulness" (Lamentations 3:22–23 ESV).

Linnea reminded me of the promise in Proverbs 19:21, that God is sovereign over the events of our lives. I reminded her of God's faithfulness to His people in the book of Daniel—and His miraculous rescues from fires and lions (Daniel 3 and 6). She shared a verse from her quiet time that promised nothing is too hard for God (Genesis 18:14).

As we encouraged each other with numerous truths from God's Word and closed our visit in prayer, gratitude, joy, and courage filled our souls.

Linnea and I aren't the only ones who draw comfort by recalling the truths about God in His Word. David the psalmist, in the midst of a fierce trial, strengthened his heart by recalling God's faithfulness and love. "If the LORD had not been my help, my soul would soon have lived in the land of silence," he wrote (Psalm 94:17 ESV). "When I thought, 'My foot slips,' your steadfast love, O LORD, held me up" (v. 18). He sought courage and bolstered his faith by meditating on what he knew about God and employed a powerful weapon to combat the discouragement that threatened to drown him.

I'm grateful for godly friends like Linnea to remind me of what I know to be true about God, but friends aren't always with us. God's Word is. On its blessed pages we find timeless truths to console and comfort our hearts.

> When the cares of my heart are many, your consolations cheer my soul.
>
> Psalm 94:19 ESV

THINK ON THIS

God cheers our weary soul with the comforts in His Word.

I praise You, God, for being mightier than my troubles, stronger than my fears, and sovereign over everything

that happens in my life. Thank You for giving us Your Word to remind us of truths that anchor us to You. When my spirit sighs and my hope grows faint, Your consolations cheer my soul.

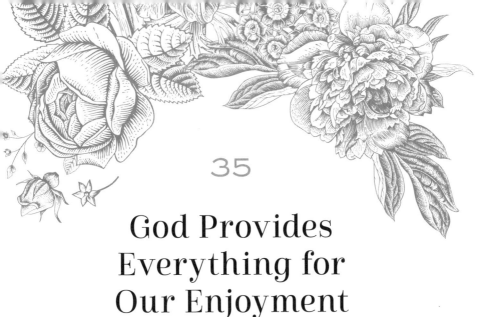

35

God Provides Everything for Our Enjoyment

I n the early days of my faith, I assumed God was a mini-malist. Verses like 1 Timothy 6:8, "But if we have food and clothing, we will be content with that" seemed to reinforce this viewpoint. God promised to provide necessities for His kids, but we shouldn't expect (or ask for) "extras."

The longer I lived, however, the more I saw evidence to the contrary. I read verses about His lavish heart and His abundant love. I looked around at the world filled with delightful things and knew God had created it. Pleasures like sunsets, nature walks, and quiet pauses made my heart happy.

One day I read past 1 Timothy 6:8 to 1 Timothy 6:17, which declares that God "richly provides us with everything *for our enjoyment*" (emphasis added). Imagine that. He filled our world with good things with us in mind.

The sunset that painted the sky pink and took your breath away? For you. That perfect spring day in the middle of winter?

Sent with you in mind. The tiny hummingbird whose daily visits to your feeder makes you smile? His idea.

On the first day of a visit with my daughter and son-in-law, I stepped into their guest room. A vase of fresh flowers adorned the nightstand. At the foot of the bed sat a basket filled with all my favorite treats. A shelf held an electric teakettle, two mugs, and a selection of herbal teas.

I never assumed these items simply appeared in my room. I knew they'd come from the hand and heart of someone who loved me and wanted to bring me joy.

So it is with the world around us. Everywhere we look, we see evidence of our Creator God who loves to bring us joy.

> Put [your] hope in God, who richly provides us with everything for our enjoyment.
>
> 1 Timothy 6:17

THINK ON THIS

God created our beautiful world for our enjoyment and His glory.

Father God, I praise You for the majesty of Your creation and the magnitude of Your genius. From the intricate details of a tiny flower to the expansive glory of the sky, Your creativity is astounding. Knowing that You fashioned it all to bring me pleasure humbles and overwhelms me. Who am I, that You would seek to bring me joy?

36

Every Life Fulfills Its Purpose

I never met my older brother, Robert Wayne. He lived for three days, yet his existence has affected my life in ways I can't describe. He is part of me. He affected Mom and Dad, too, who later impacted me. One day, I'll meet him in heaven, and his life will continue to impact me for all eternity.

If we've lived long enough, we've been touched by an "untimely" death. A baby dies in utero. A teen dies in a car accident. A young mother succumbs to cancer.

We wrestle with the whys and question God's purposes. Sometimes we doubt God's love. Psalm 57:2 comforts me when thoughts like these attack my faith. "I cry out to God Most High, to God who fulfills his purpose for me" (ESV).

This verse and others like it (Job 42:2, Philippians 1:6) remind me that every life has a purpose, and God will fulfill His purpose for it. The baby in the womb had just as much purpose as the senior saint, who lived to be one hundred. God weighs the value of a life by its existence, not by its longevity.

When a person dies, either in their mother's womb, their father's arms, or at a hundred years old surrounded by loved ones, we can know they've fulfilled the purpose for which God created them. We can trust their death was not untimely, nor was their life wasted.

Some days I grieve what life would have been like if my brother had lived. I wonder this about other family members and friends I've lost too soon. When I question why their lives were shorter than I'd hoped, I bring my sorrow to God and weep into His chest. He holds me close and whispers, "No eye has seen, no ear has heard, and no mind has imagined what God has prepared for those who love him." (1 Corinthians 2:9 NLT).

"You can trust me."

> I cry out to God Most High, to God who fulfills his purpose for me.
>
> Psalm 57:2 ESV

THINK ON THIS

We can take comfort from knowing that, short or long, each life has purpose and meaning.

Father, thank You for the comfort You provide when I grieve. Knowing that You have ordained the number of our days and the purpose for each life shields my heart from bitterness. I praise You for declaring that even the

shortest life has value. As I seek to glorify You with every day You grant me, show me the way. I love You, Father. I trust You, even when I don't understand.

37

It's Simple to Have a Relationship with God

I've filled out more than a few job applications in my lifetime. Each form asks me for my personal information, previous job experience, and noteworthy skills. The last section usually requires me to list people of influence who can vouch for my character and abilities.

I've never listed a toddler in this section of a job application.

You probably haven't, either. Young children aren't exactly credible witnesses. They're not usually well connected, either. They hold no political, economic, or social power, nor are they known for their business acumen. They're just little children—simple, trusting, and transparent.

I suspect this is why Jesus chose a little child to describe what we must be like to have a relationship with God.

"Jesus called a little child to him and put the child among them. Then he said, 'I tell you the truth, unless you turn from your sins and become like little children, you will never get into the Kingdom of Heaven. So anyone who becomes as humble as this little child is the greatest in the Kingdom of Heaven'" (Matthew 18:2–4 NLT).

When grown-ups come to faith in Christ, we complicate everything. We think we have to clean up our behavior, act a certain way, or pray lofty prayers to obtain salvation. If we do all the right things (whatever we think they may be), we can convince God to love us.

It sounds good, except this isn't what Jesus said.

He said we must become like children.

Think about the last toddler you cared for. They were needy and helpless. They depended on you for everything and trusted you implicitly (unless you tried to feed them broccoli). And they loved you—sincerely and without pretense.

This is all God asks of us. To acknowledge that we are needy and hopeless without Him. To trust that He's done everything for our salvation. And to love Him with our whole hearts in gratitude.

If you've never trusted Christ as your Savior, today can be the day. Turn to page 183 for more information about how to have a relationship with God. If you have trusted Christ, will you join me in committing to come to God every day in childlike faith and trust?

> I tell you the truth, unless you turn from your sins and become like little children, you will never get into the Kingdom of Heaven.
>
> Matthew 18:3 NLT

THINK ON THIS

Faith is a gift of God. When we come to Him as helpless as a child, we can fling ourselves on Him, knowing He will catch us.

Father, thank You for making it simple to have a relationship with You. I praise You for accepting us just where we are. Help us remain childlike in our faith, trust You for everything, and love You with all our hearts. In Jesus's name I pray, amen.

38

God Lifts Our Eyes to His Creation

Mrs. Phillips spent forty years of her life as an elementary school teacher. Parents and children love her, and I know why. She's never lost her youthful attitude. Although her hair has grayed and her movements slowed, her spirit has remained childlike.

I met her walking through the neighborhood one spring day.

"Isn't this an absolutely delicious day?" she asked, clasping her hands together and smiling as if it were her birthday.

I'd been slogging along, trying to get my customary three miles in before lunchtime, but when I saw the delight that bubbled out of Mrs. Phillips, I stopped and looked around.

Bright sunshine filtered through newly budding trees, warming my skin. Birds chattered in the treetops like old friends at a high school reunion. The scent of wisteria and tea olive wafted around us—heaven's perfume.

Mrs. Phillips was right. It was an absolutely *delicious* day.

And I had almost missed it.

Mrs. Phillips took a page out of David the psalmist's songbook.

He also walked through the world with his eyes open, looking for God's gifts. "When I look at your heavens, the work of your fingers, the moon and the stars, which you have set in place," he wrote, lifting the Israelites eyes to the majesty of God's creation" (Psalm 8:3 ESV).

In Psalm 104:25, he directed their gaze to the ocean, "Here is the sea, great and wide, which teems with creatures innumerable, living things both small and great" (ESV).

In Psalm 34:8, he encouraged the congregation to "taste and see that the LORD is good."

I'm often guilty of whooshing past marvelous aspects of our world without giving their Creator a second thought.

I wonder how much more grateful my heart would be if I'd slow down, look around, and praise God for the gifts He surrounds us with every day.

I invite you to join me in taking time to savor the delights God fills our world with.

Because today is an absolutely delicious day.

> This is the day that the LORD has made; let us rejoice and be glad in it.
>
> Psalm 118:24 ESV

THINK ON THIS

God fills our world with delights.

Father, You fill our world with good things—sights to delight our eyes, sounds to fill our ears, and scents to make our noses tingle. You are a grand and glorious Creator. I worship You. Thank You for enabling us to experience the joy of Your creation every day. Amen.

39

God Promises to Help Us

When my husband and I were expecting our first daughter, we received a lot of advice. Friends, acquaintances, and strangers who eyed my burgeoning belly said things like, "Parenting is the hardest thing you'll ever do," and, "Life will never be the same." Others smiled knowingly and declared, "Sometimes you'll just want to die. But really, children are great. I promise."

The closer we came to my delivery date, the more frightened I became. *What have we done?* I wondered. *What makes me think I can feed, nurture, and raise a helpless human being?*

The thought of shepherding her spiritual training was even more daunting. How will we know what to say? Her eternal destiny depends on an accurate understanding of God. What if we mess it up?

One Sunday morning, I struggled to concentrate on the pastor's sermon. My mind whirled, and my stomach (already prone to acid reflux) churned with a thousand fears. Then I spotted Mrs. B. across the sanctuary. Mrs. B. loved the Lord and had reared five children. I could talk with her.

As soon as the pastor said, "Amen," I waddled to her side. "Mrs. B.," I blurted, "I'm afraid I'm going to be a terrible mother." Tears streamed from my eyes as I shared every fear that haunted me.

She led me to a pew, sat beside me, and patted my shoulder. "Oh honey," she said, "You don't need be afraid. God knows you can't do this alone. He will help you." Seventeen words, but she said them with such certainty that I believed her.

And you know what? She was right. God did help me. Wisdom didn't come automatically. David and I had to seek it from the Bible, wise friends, and sound resources. We sought God's help in every situation we encountered, and He directed our paths.

Our two daughters (yes, we went through it all a second time) now have families of their own. Whenever they grow frightened or overwhelmed, I remember Mrs. B. I sit them down, hug them, and remind them, "You don't need to be afraid. God knows you can't do this alone. He will help you."

> For I am the LORD your God who takes hold of your right hand and says to you, Do not fear; I will help you.
>
> Isaiah 41:13

THINK ON THIS

You don't need to be afraid. God knows you can't do this alone. He will help you.

Father, thank You for the fears that drive me to You. I praise You that before I encounter a challenge, You already know it. You promise to walk every step of the way with me, hold my hand, and help me. I need not fear, for You are with me.

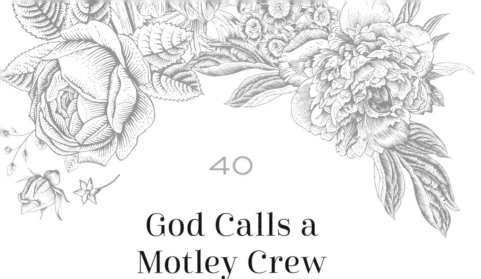

40

God Calls a Motley Crew

In the early 1980s, some of my friends listened to a heavy metal band called Motley Crue. I've never been a fan, but the band's name sometimes comes to mind when I think about the people who make up God's family. The apostle Paul describes us this way: "Not many of you were wise by human standards; not many were influential; not many were of noble birth" (1 Corinthians 1:26).

In the churches I've attended, I've heard individuals addicted to drugs, alcohol, or harmful behavior like theft proclaim to the world how Jesus saved them. My friend Jimmy, now an ordained minister, spent forty years in jail for murdering a man during a bank robbery. Others of us with less-checkered pasts might struggle with different challenges—we lack intelligence, pedigree, or money.

This motley crew God calls the church isn't a twenty-first century phenomenon. God has always chosen, as Paul noted, "the foolish things of the world to shame the wise" and "the weak things of the world to shame the strong" (v. 27).

Except for the first man and woman, who were, indeed, perfect, God has adopted into His family those who lied habitually (Jacob), acted cowardly (Gideon), denigrated women (Samson), and sold themselves for money (Rahab). He's used people who were too young (Timothy), too old (Abraham), and too short (Zacchaeus).

Moses stuttered, Martha worried, and the Samaritan woman was divorced (more than once). He even "chose the lowly things of this world and the despised things," like those suffering from leprosy and demon possession and those ostracized, like tax collectors, to become His children (v. 28).

Whenever I feel less than, I look around and realize I'm in good company. Occasionally, God calls someone with extraordinary talent or ability, but most of us are rather ordinary.

You know why?

"So that no one may boast before him" (v. 29).

If I thought God called me because I was smart, pretty, or gifted, I'd be tempted to brag. "Look at me! Isn't God lucky to have me on His team?" I'd steal God's glory faster than squirrels swipe nuts at a peanut festival.

But God's Word reminds us that without His empowering, we could do absolutely nothing that matters for eternity.

God planned it this way so He—not us—gets the glory.

God's family is indeed a motley crew. And this is a good thing. A proper perspective of ourselves will help keep us humble—and grateful.

> Brothers and sisters, think of what you were when you were called. Not many of you were wise by human standards; not many were influential; not many were of noble

birth. But God chose the foolish things of the world to shame the wise.

1 Corinthians 1:26–27

THINK ON THIS

God called a motley crew to Himself and refines us for His glory.

Father, I don't deserve to be one of Your children, yet You welcomed me into Your family. You saved me and changed me, and now You call me to work alongside You in Your kingdom. Help me remember that anything good in me comes only from You. Take the meager loaves and fishes of my talents and multiply them for Your glory. In the precious name of Jesus, I ask, amen.

41

God Draws Near

Have you ever approached someone who acted as if they wanted to get as far away from you as possible?

It happens to me from time to time with patients in our dental office. They make an appointment, check in at the front desk, and follow me to my dental chair, yet they clearly wish they were somewhere else. I suspect their desire to avoid me has more to do with my sharp instruments than my charming personality, but you never know.

Most people don't work in a dental office, but I trust they can still relate to the feeling of rejection. Remember that classmate in sixth grade you so desperately wanted to become friends with? The one that avoided you at lunchtime and took the long way home so she wouldn't have to walk with you? Or that coworker who seemed so fun, yet despite your efforts, never let you get close? Or that adult child who resists your efforts to spend time together and changes the subject when you talk about anything personal?

Rejection hurts, no matter where it comes from. It causes us to doubt our worth and wonder what's wrong with us. Thankfully, we need not fear God will reject us. James 4:8 (ESV) tells us, "Draw near to God and he will draw near to you."

Every step we take toward Him prompts Him to move closer. When we study our Bible to learn more about Him, He reveals new aspects of Himself. When we seek His comfort, He opens His arms wide.

We don't have to perform, impress, or earn His companionship. He offers it freely and wholeheartedly. "Come to me, all you who are weary and burdened, and I will give you rest," Jesus said in Matthew 11:28. He issued the same invitation in Revelation 22:17: "Let the one who is thirsty come." With these marvelous invitations, we can approach Him with confidence, knowing He'll always respond.

> Draw near to God, and he will draw near to you.
>
> James 4:8 ESV

THINK ON THIS

We need not fear that God will reject us. If we draw near to God, He will draw near to us.

Father, You are my sure and constant hope, a forever presence in my life. Though all others may reject me, You never will. Oh, how my heart takes comfort in this thought. Your Word promises that when I take the first step toward You, no matter how far I've wandered, You immediately draw near. Thank You, kind Father. I love You so much.

42

God Never Changes

"Okay, kids," I called, "time for lunch." My four grandchildren scampered in and gathered around the table, jostling and squirming like puppies around a food bowl.

"But Gigi," Andrew announced, looking at the plates I'd so carefully prepared, "we don't like chicken nuggets."

"Since when? You told me last week they were your favorite lunch food."

"I don't know," he shrugged. "We just don't like 'em anymore."

Anyone who's tried to keep up with small children's food preferences can feel my pain. That day, it was simple enough to pull out the peanut butter and honey and offer an alternative, but sometimes people change in more serious ways.

A faithful husband breaks his marriage vows. A loyal friend doesn't want to hang out anymore. A reliable advisor mismanages a trust. People change—and not always for the better.

When others disappoint us, we can take great comfort in knowing God never changes. Moses told the Israelites, "The LORD your God is God; he is the faithful God, keeping his covenant of love to a thousand generations of those who love him and keep his commandments" (Deuteronomy 7:9).

A thousand generations. That's a long time.

The author of Hebrews wrote that Jesus, God in the flesh, "is the same yesterday and today and forever" (Hebrews 13:8).

Forever is a long time.

God is the ultimate bridegroom, promising to love and cherish us for better or for worse, in sickness and in health, in poverty and in wealth, so long as we both shall live. Which is into eternity.

Even if we fail Him, He loves us still. When our faith grows weak, He remains faithful. When all others forsake us, He stays by our side (Deuteronomy 31:6). He cannot act outside of His character—good, patient, kind, pure, loving, and forgiving.

"'Though the mountains be shaken and the hills be removed, yet my unfailing love for you will not be shaken nor my covenant of peace be removed,' says the LORD, who has compassion on you" (Isaiah 54:10).

People can change. Chicken nuggets may fall out of favor. But our God remains the same forever.

And forever's a really long time.

Jesus is the same yesterday and today and forever.

Hebrews 13:8

THINK ON THIS

Even if all others change, we can take comfort in knowing that God never will.

In a world that changes every day, thank You, precious God, for being a solid and sure hope I can cling to. When the winds of trials blow me off course, You are there to catch me—every time. When I wonder who I can trust, I'm grateful I can look to You in confidence and faith. I never have to worry that You'll fail me, forget me, or forsake me. I trust You. Amen.

43

God Shares Our Grief

Six-year-old me chose Speedy the Turtle from a pet-store display full of little green reptiles. My sister Cindy chose Pokey, his sibling. The four of us enjoyed many hours of happy play. We rearranged their habitat at least once a day, held turtle races, and fed them lettuce, apples, and the occasional pill bug scavenged from the yard.

One day, I noticed Speedy the Turtle wasn't so speedy. In fact, he wasn't moving at all. That day was the first time death wrapped its icy fingers around my young heart.

My friend Laura helped me prepare for the funeral. As I nestled Speedy into a cotton-lined box that had once held one of Mom's bracelets, Laura tucked yellow beads "to match his stripes" around his body. Together, we picked dandelions to decorate his grave. After we pushed the rocky New England soil over the box, we shared a teary hug and a Three Musketeers bar she'd saved "for an emergency."

I wish all my grown-up tears could be soothed with a hug and a candy bar. When illness, grief, uncertainty, and trials elbow their way into my life, I can lose perspective and wonder if others care. Sometimes I wonder if God cares. Isaiah 53:4 reminds me He does: "Surely he took up our pain and bore our suffering." He is present in every grief and sees every tear I shed.

When I go to Him in prayer and seek comfort in His Word, His peace settles over my soul. I need not fear I'm overburdening Him with the multitude of my concerns. His shoulders are broad, and His heart is kind.

The truth I find in the Bible wraps me in the warmest hug. His promises become, as the psalmist described, "sweeter than honey" (Psalm 119:103). His love for me shores up my wavering trust.

Sometimes, in the multitude of His mercies, my difficult circumstances change. But even when they don't, God assures me He will carry my sorrows and share my grief. I'll never face them alone. The comfort of His presence soothes my heart and cheers my soul.

> Surely he took up our pain and bore our suffering.
>
> Isaiah 53:4

THINK ON THIS

God's presence cheers our hearts better than a hug and a candy bar.

I praise You, Father, for the comfort You provide when life overwhelms me. When my heart aches with sorrow

or races with fear, I can come to You in prayer, and You hear me. You walk through every trial with me. You speak to me through the still, small voice of Your Holy Spirit and the resounding voice of Your Word. In the embrace of Your presence, my heart sings again.

44

God Is Not Only with Us, He's in Us

Do you ever envy the ancient Israelites? I do. Every time I read the account of the exodus, I feel a wee bit jealous. When God led His people out of Egypt to the promised land, He declared His presence would go with them.

He appeared to the Israelites as a pillar of cloud by day and a pillar of fire by night (Numbers 9:15–17). When Moses built the tabernacle, God's presence dwelled between the cherubim in the holy of holies (Exodus 25:22). On the day Solomon dedicated the temple, God's presence so filled the structure that the priests couldn't minister there (2 Chronicles 7:1–2).

Sadly, Scripture also records God's presence leaving the temple because of the nation's sin (Ezekiel 10). Other accounts describe how God's Spirit came and went from Old Testament believers (1 Samuel 16:14, Judges 16:20).

Jesus, however, promised a new way to experience God's presence—the gift of the Holy Spirit. For those who have placed our faith in Christ, God, in the person of the Holy Spirit, lives in us forever (John 14:16–17).

He teaches us (John 14:26), prays for us (Romans 8:26), empowers us (Acts 1:8), and guides us into all truth (John 16:13). Best of all, He guarantees our salvation. "When you believed, you were marked in him with a seal, the promised Holy Spirit, who is a deposit guaranteeing our inheritance until the redemption of those who are God's possession" (Ephesians 1:13–14).

I'm so grateful we don't need to fear God's presence will depart from us. In the person of the Holy Spirit, He is not only *with* us, He is *in* us. And He will never leave us.

Maybe we shouldn't envy the Israelites after all. We have something better.

> I will ask the Father, and he will give you another advocate to help you and be with you forever—the Spirit of truth. The world cannot accept him, because it neither sees him nor knows him. But you know him, for he lives with you and will be in you.
>
> John 14:16–17

THINK ON THIS

God is not only *with* us, He is *in* us. And He will never leave us.

I praise You, Father, for the gift of Your Holy Spirit. Because of His abiding presence within me, I am never alone. I don't need visible manifestations of You—I have

You. Thank You for the many times You've made Your presence known to me. I praise You for the still, small voice that teaches me, prays for me, empowers me, and guards me until my salvation is complete. I love You so much.

45

Aging Comes with a Promise

Seven-year-old Caroline runs like a brown-eyed doe bounding through the forest on a sunny day. Her feet are light, and her movements graceful. She can sprint down the beach and back with her Papa and exclaim, "That was fun. Let's do it again." Papa, breathing like he'd just raced a seven-year-old and lost, isn't so sure.

Five-year-old Andrew and three-year-old Collin wrestle like puppies in a pen. They twist, strain, and tumble. Occasionally, when they put a little too much force behind their fun, one will yelp, but for the most part, they bounce up effortlessly from a tumbling match.

Nine-year-old Lauren swims like an otter, sometimes a mile before breakfast, then frolics at the trampoline park. As 10 p.m. approaches, my eyelids droop and my thinking becomes fuzzy, but she bubbles with fresh ideas and conversation.

Every day our grandchildren's bodies grow in strength and endurance. Not David's and mine. Despite our best efforts at physical fitness, we sometimes feel twinges in our knees. My vision requires stronger contact lenses. Words like *sciatica*, *arthritis*, and *osteopenia* creep into our conversations. Whether we accept it or not, our bodies are aging.

Perhaps the apostle Paul felt a little like we do after a day with our grandkids. As he declared solid reasons to believe in the resurrection from the dead, he commented on what will happen to our bodies when our earthly life ends (1 Corinthians 15:42–44).

Our earthly bodies must die for our heavenly bodies to live forever. The perishable must return to the ground so our spirits can live with Christ. As our mortal bodies crumble like ancient parchment, our spiritual bodies rise from the dust.

The youth and vigor of children remind us of what we were but are no longer. Paul's words to the Corinthians remind us of what we will be someday. Imperishable. Glorious. Powerful. Each ache and pain ushers us a tiny bit closer to this incredible reality.

Maybe aging isn't so bad after all.

> So will it be with the resurrection of the dead. The body that is sown is perishable, it is raised imperishable; it is sown in dishonor, it is raised in glory; it is sown in weakness, it is raised in power; it is sown a natural body, it is raised a spiritual body.
>
> 1 Corinthians 15:42–44

THINK ON THIS

Aging isn't to be mourned. It's to be celebrated. Each year brings us closer to the day when we will leave our frail humanity and clothe ourselves in immortality.

Father, I seldom view getting older as a blessing, but when I realize that each year (and each ache and pain) brings me closer to the day when I'll live forever in Your presence, perhaps it is. Thank You that I can look forward to the day when I receive my new body and will live forever in Your presence.

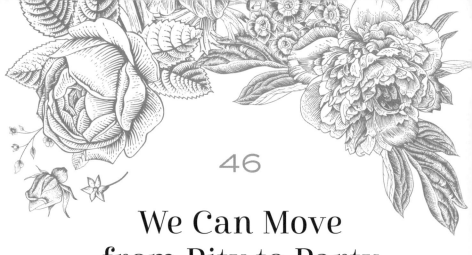

46

We Can Move from Pity to Party When We Praise

When was the last time you had a good, old-fashioned pity party? Complete with moans, groans, and more tears than a toddler in time-out? I'm normally upbeat, but every once and a while, I descend into what author John Bunyan called the *Slough of Despond*.

Apparently, I'm in good company. Psalm 13:1–2 records one of David's prayers during a season of discouragement. "How long, LORD? Will you forget me forever? How long will you hide your face from me? How long must I wrestle with my thoughts and day after day have sorrow in my heart? How long will my enemy triumph over me?"

It comforts me to know that even "a man after God's own heart" struggled sometimes. More than proving that misery loves company, David's words give me a strategy to fight discouragement. David came before God with honesty and vulnerability, and God invites us to follow David's example.

Listen to what he said after he voiced his complaint to God:

"But I trust in your unfailing love; my heart rejoices in your salvation. I will sing the Lord's praise, for he has been good to me" (vv. 5–6).

David didn't hide his feelings. That would have been pointless, since God knows everyone's thoughts. But after he expressed his pain, David didn't wallow in it. Instead, he turned his mind to God's goodness. His song of lament became a song of faith, praise, and thanksgiving.

"I trust you," he declared in this passage, both to God and to his own heart. "I'm grateful you saved me. I can sing your praises, because you have been so good to me."

We can do the same. Instead of letting trouble discourage us, we can declare by faith that God is worthy of our trust, we can rejoice in our salvation, and we can sing God's praises to the listening world. When we do, we turn our pity into a party by banishing discouragement and embracing joy.

Truly, God has been good to us.

> I will sing the Lord's praise, for he has been good to me.
>
> Psalm 13:6

THINK ON THIS

We can move from pity to party when we praise.

Lord, You alone are worthy of praise. In the words of David, Your love is unfailing. I can't comprehend that You would save me, and yet You did. You have been so

good to me—far better than I deserve. I choose to focus on Your goodness, instead of my trials. Be glorified in me today.

47

We'll Share Heaven with Those We Love

A few years ago, my daughter and I went back home. Home for me is Bristol, Rhode Island, a tiny town on Narragansett Bay. Although Mary Leigh was born in South Carolina, she shares my love for my birthplace.

We rode electric bikes on the East Bay Bike Path and enjoyed Del's frozen lemonade from a sidewalk stand in Barrington. We stopped at Vienna Bakery for Bismarck pastries, Italian bread, and crème horns. One day we ate Thai food, seafood, and Portuguese doughnuts.

Our visit to Newport ended with a stroll on the Cliff Walk and a tour of the Vanderbilt mansion, The Breakers. In between, I showed her Rogers Free Library, where I checked out my first library book; the route where I delivered newspapers in a blizzard; and the little Primitive Methodist church where I memorized John 3:16 in vacation Bible school.

I could have visited these places alone, but my joy was magnified because I shared it with my daughter.

I suspect one of the sweetest parts of heaven will be sharing it with those we love. First Corinthians 13:12 reveals that when we get to heaven, we'll not only recognize our believing loved ones, we'll know each other fully. "For now we see only a reflection as in a mirror; then we shall see face to face. Now I know in part; then I shall know fully, even as I am fully known." When Jesus rose from the dead in His glorified body, His disciples and loved ones recognized him (John 20:16, 27–28). Five hundred witnesses did, too (1 Corinthians 15:6). Because we'll have glorified bodies like Jesus, we'll also be recognizable—fully recognizable. This means others will see us as we really are, untainted by our sinful nature and the emotional, physical, and spiritual scars of our lives on earth. Once we recognize each other, we'll be free to experience the joys of heaven together.

Maybe those who went to heaven first will spot us from a distance, rush to grab our hands, and show us around. We'll tour the celestial mansion Jesus has prepared for us and walk the streets of gold—together. Maybe we'll even eat Portuguese doughnuts.

I'm so grateful, when we see each other face-to-face in heaven, we'll know each other, love each other, and explore the joys of heaven—together.

> For now we see only a reflection as in a mirror; then we shall see face to face. Now I know in part; then I shall know fully, even as I am fully known.
>
> 1 Corinthians 13:12

THINK ON THIS

In heaven, we'll know each other, love each other, and explore the joys of heaven—together.

Precious Savior, I can only imagine what heaven will be like. Everything You've promised and so much more. I praise You that although our new bodies will be different, they'll still be recognizable to those we love. The joy of being fully known and experiencing heaven together— with our loved ones and with You—will make our joy complete. What a glorious God You are.

48

God Uses Our Inadequacies to Bring Him Glory

Have you heard the term *glory stealer*? Glory stealers are people who try to steal the honor, praise, attention, or worship that belongs to God and claim it for themselves. This is a serious sin, because God (rightly so) shares His glory with no one. "I am the Lord; that is my name! I will not yield my glory to another" (Isaiah 42:8).

Turns out the Bible describes quite a few glory stealers. Satan was the first (are you surprised?). He tried to steal God's glory by exalting himself above God (Isaiah 14:12–15). Wicked King Herod followed in Satan's slimy footsteps when he allowed his subjects to venerate him to the level of a god (Acts 12:23).

But fallen angels and pompous kings aren't the only glory stealers. Sometimes ordinary people like you and me take credit for what only God can do.

Consider Moses. He was a stuttering shepherd when God called him. Yet He stole God's glory by taking credit for what God did—brought water from a rock (Numbers 20:11).

Because God knows our tendency to exalt ourselves instead of Him, He gave us a gift—the gift of frail and flawed humanity. The apostle Paul describes it this way: "But we have this treasure in jars of clay to show that this all-surpassing power is from God and not from us" (2 Corinthians 4:7).

Have you ever felt inadequate to do the work God has called you to do? Maybe you're not very attractive, educated, or articulate. You struggle to do things others accomplish easily.

This is a gift! Our humanity, our ordinary-ness is a blessed treasure to remind us not to steal God's glory. Whenever He calls us to do something for Him, we know it didn't happen because *we* are so wonderful, but because *He* is so wonderful.

Any shortcoming that humbles us and requires us to depend more fully on God can make us glory givers instead of glory stealers. This is a marvelous thing. The Westminster Catechism begins with these words, "Man's chief end is to glorify God, and to enjoy him forever."

We do this best by serving, speaking, and witnessing fully aware that we are jars of clay.

> But we have this treasure in jars of clay to show that this all-surpassing power is from God and not from us.
>
> 2 Corinthians 4:7

THINK ON THIS

God gives us the gift of flawed and frail humanity to help us become glory givers, not glory stealers.

Oh, Father, I never thought I'd praise You for creating my shortcomings, inadequacies, and flaws, but here I am. Anything that makes me rely more fully on You and not myself is a gift. A marvelous gift. A glorious gift. Thank You. I surrender every one of my insufficiencies to You and ask You to use me, despite myself, to bring You glory. In the name of the Lord, Jesus Christ, I pray, amen.

49

Jesus Brings Peace

I was too young to be a hippie, but I found them fascinating. While my friends and I wore ponytails and jumpers, the high school- and college-aged girls wore long hair and flowing clothing, tie-dye and fringe. They greeted each other with a nod and a two-fingered peace sign. If *cool* had a look, they owned it.

One day, I found a treasure on the playground—a leather band with a peace sign on it. I tied it around my head and wore it for days—until my mother made me take it off for church.

The search for peace isn't unique to the seventies. People have been looking for peace since time began. Diplomats broker peace accords. Therapists counsel spouses attempting to reconcile. Fretful souls try drugs, alcohol, food, meditation, shopping, or exercise to find a sense of calm in a turbulent world.

Saint Augustine rightly described the human condition when he said, "You have made us for yourself, and our heart is restless until it finds its rest in you."[11]

Isaiah knew what God knew—that He would one day

send the Messiah to restore the peace sin destroyed. Under inspiration of God, he called this deliverer the Prince of Peace (Isaiah 9:6). The apostle Paul said of Jesus. "For he himself is our peace" (Ephesians 2:14).

"Peace I leave with you;" Jesus told His disciples, "my peace I give you. I do not give to you as the world gives. Do not let your hearts be troubled and do not be afraid" (John 14:27).

Only in Jesus can we find true and lasting peace—with God, with others, and with ourselves. The hippies who discovered it sparked the Jesus Movement of the late sixties and early seventies.

When we surrender our life to God's control, His peace protects our heart. It sustains us during times of trial, comforts us when we grieve, and, one day, will allow us to stand reconciled before God, unashamed and unafraid.

> I have told you these things, so that in me [Jesus] you may have peace.
>
> John 16:33

THINK ON THIS

When we surrender our life to God's control, His peace protects our heart.

Father, Psalm 46:2 declares, "We will not fear, though the earth give way and the mountains fall into the heart of the sea." Sometimes I feel like the mountains

of my life are falling into the sea, but Your peace brings calm to my chaos. Remind me, every day, to put on the bulletproof vest of peace and allow it to guard my heart and mind. Amen.

50

When God Saves Us, He Recreates Us

My husband, David, and I have two very different before-Christ stories. When David met Jesus, he was a seventeen-year-old alcohol and drug user. I was an eighteen-year-old type A honor student. He sought joy and fulfillment in bottles, pills, and friends. I looked for it in accomplishments, goals, and accolades. Although we walked very different paths, our hearts were agonizingly similar.

In His mercy, God drew us to Himself and transformed us. I'm not talking about sanctification, the gradual changes that happen throughout our Christian life. I'm talking about how God changed the very essence of who we were—instantly—at the moment of salvation. Second Corinthians 5:17 (ESV) describes it this way: "If anyone is in Christ, he is [not becomes] a new creation. The old has passed away; behold, the new has come."

When God saves us, He gives us a new heart—His heart. Ezekiel recorded how God describes this process: "I will give you a new heart, and a new spirit I will put within you. And I will remove the heart of stone from your flesh and give you a heart of flesh" (36:26 ESV).

Almost immediately, David noticed that his attitude toward sin had changed. When he behaved in ways that dishonored the Lord, he felt differently—sad and ashamed instead of arrogantly rebellious. My attitude changed, too. Instead of being self-focused, I found myself caring about the things God cared about. We both noticed a hunger to read God's Word and gather with God's people.

These attitudes and desires weren't natural for us. They were supernatural evidence of the transformation God had done in our lives.

If you've placed your faith in Christ, you are a new creation, too. Rejoice in this. Embrace your new identity. Walk in newness of life.

> Therefore, if anyone is in Christ, he is a new creation. The old has passed away; behold, the new has come.
>
> 2 Corinthians 5:17 ESV

THINK ON THIS

When God saves us, He recreates us. Behold, the new has come!

Father God, I'm so grateful You didn't just rescue me from spending eternity in hell. You transformed me into someone with the potential to bring You glory. You

removed my stony heart and replaced it with one that beats with Your love. You transformed my mind so I could love what You love and hate what You hate. You gave me the ability to glorify You with my life. Thank You, precious Father.

51

God Sends Laughter to Cheer Our Hearts

Christmas 2009 was the saddest holiday in our family's history. My brother-in-law, Luther, was dying. Doctors had given him weeks to live, and we knew this would be our last Christmas with him on this side of eternity. He'd been in bed all week, but he rallied his strength to join us around the Christmas tree.

It was supposed to be the most wonderful time of the year, but the presents and food had lost their sparkle. Conversation lagged. Despite the tree's glow, a shadow hovered over our celebration. Several of us had to leave the room to wipe away tears.

Even our normally riotous white elephant gift exchange fell flat. Until my teenage daughter unwrapped a book—*The Three Little Wolves and the Big Bad Pig*, a hilarious parody of the traditional children's story.

She read the first few pages aloud, using different voices for each character. Someone giggled. Encouraged, she read on, growing more animated and sillier with each turn of the page. Then my sister-in-law laughed. The contagious sound infected us all.

By the end of the book, everyone, including Luther, was wiping tears from our eyes—but this time they were tears of laughter. Ecclesiastes 3:1, 4 describes what we experienced: "There is a time for everything . . . a time to weep and a time to laugh."

When Luther went home to be with the Lord, we wept, but we didn't weep for him. He was healthy and whole again. We cried because we couldn't imagine our family without his silent strength and tender heart.

Yet, as God had done that Christmas, He sprinkled our grief with times of laughter. We remembered Luther's corny jokes, his love for his nieces and nephews, and his passion for the Baltimore Colts. And we smiled at the memory of our family gathered around the Christmas tree laughing over a children's book about three little wolves and a big bad pig.

If you're struggling with a spirit of heaviness today, I encourage you to reflect on the laughable moments of your life. Smile at the memories. Watch a funny video. Tell someone your favorite joke. Or read a silly book. I guarantee you'll be laughing soon.

> There is a time for everything, and a season for every activity under the heavens . . . a time to weep and a time to laugh.
>
> Ecclesiastes 3:1, 4

THINK ON THIS

God's precious gift of laughter lifts the heart and cheers the soul.

Father, life can be so serious. Thank You for creating us with the ability to laugh. I praise You for filling our world with sights and experiences that lift our spirits and make our hearts smile. When our hearts feel broken—or just tired and discouraged—give us eyes to see the funny things around us. Fill our mouths with laughter and our eyes with happy tears. In Jesus's name I pray, amen.

52

God's Word Is the Sweetest Food of All

When the server asked me, "Would you like some dessert?" I vacillated. My love for all things delicious wanted to scream, "Yes!" My desire to guard my health (and my weight) said, "Maybe." My follow-up question, "What's the special?" and her answer, "White chocolate raspberry cake," settled it.

"Yes, please!"

Still aware (in a guilty sort of way) of the calorie and sugar content, I nibbled at the bottom layer—cake with a mediocre custard filling. *Not worth the calories.* I moved to the top layer—same white cake, but slathered in a raspberry jam, topped with cream cheese icing, and sprinkled with white chocolate curls. *Oh yeah, now we're talking.* I ate the entire top layer, scraped the last smidgen of icing off the plate, and licked my fork clean.

I'm ashamed to admit that for years, I approached Bible consumption the same way. The first year I attempted to read the Bible through, the luscious details of creation, Abraham's

156

call, and Jacob's family fed my spiritual taste buds. The contents of Exodus did the same. But Leviticus tasted strange and, in some places, off-putting. *Lots of blood and fatty lobes of liver. Not worth my time.* I flipped to the New Testament, where I found sweet accounts of miracles, meals, and messages of God's love. *Now we're talking.*

Instead of having a discriminating palate, I had an immature and untrained one. Second Timothy 3:16 reminds us, "*All* Scripture is God-breathed and useful" (emphasis added), not just the tastiest parts.

But one year I persevered and read the whole Bible through. Instead of picking and choosing, I learned God calls us to feast on all the riches of His Word. When we do, we discover the truth, power, and deliciousness in its many layers. As pastor A. W. Tozer declared, "Nothing less than a whole Bible makes a whole Christian."[12]

> How sweet are your words to my taste, sweeter than honey to my mouth!
>
> Psalm 119:103

THINK ON THIS

The entirety of God's Word will delight and satisfy us.

Father, I praise You for inspiring every word of the Bible and using it to help us become the men and women You created us to be—faith-filled, fearless,

and faithful. Thank You for helping me develop a taste for reading it. Draw me to it every day so You can nourish my soul.

53

God Protects and Instructs His Children

One of the Bible's greatest strengths is that it records an unedited history of Israel and the early church. Unlike modern-day propaganda, which airbrushes its leaders and whitewashes its facts, the Bible doesn't hide foolish mistakes, wanton sin, and poor choices. It tells the truth.

Why?

Like a letter from a wise father to his child, the Bible serves as God's instruction manual—if we're smart enough to learn from it. Paul's letter to the Corinthian church explains why God's inspired Word records our spiritual ancestors' good and bad choices: "These things happened to them [the Israelites] as examples and were written down as warnings for us" (1 Corinthians 10:11).

Examples and warnings.

God, the ultimate loving Father, doesn't send His kids into the world defenseless. Instead, He counsels us through His Word. "His divine power has given us everything we need for a godly life through our knowledge of him who called us by his own glory and goodness" (2 Peter 1:3).

We don't have to experience the life-wrecking power of lust. We can learn from King David's heartbreaking example (2 Samuel 11). We don't have to wonder what might happen if we obey some, but not all, of God's instructions. Solomon's story shows how ignoring God's commands can set in motion an avalanche of consequences (1 Kings 11:1–13). Israel's infatuation with the world (1 Samuel 8:4–22), Gehazi's greed (2 Kings 5:20–27), and Lot's compromise (Jude 1:7–8; also see Genesis 13:10; 14:12; 19:1) echo through the ages as disasters to avoid and warnings to heed.

We love to read about Red Sea rescues and graveyard resurrections. They make us feel faith-filled and triumphant. The sad stories don't fill us with joy, but they should fill us with gratitude. We can be thankful God loves us enough to tell us the truth, warn us away from sin, and teach us His principles.

The author of Proverbs captured God's Father heart toward us when he wrote, "My son, pay attention to what I say; turn your ear to my words. Do not let them out of your sight, keep them within your heart; for they are life to those who find them and health to one's whole body" (4:20–22).

> These things happened to them as examples and were written down as warnings for us.
>
> 1 Corinthians 10:11

THINK ON THIS

Our Father God doesn't send His children into the world defenseless. He provides His Word to guide and protect us.

I praise You, precious Father, for providing everything I need to navigate this life successfully. Within the pages of Your Word, I find truth, wisdom, and instruction. Thank You for helping me learn from my spiritual ancestors and avoid the sin and heartbreak they experienced. I praise You for including happy stories, too, of faith-filled men and women who followed You wholeheartedly. Make me like them, Father God, for Your glory.

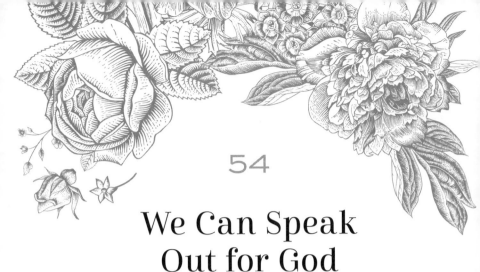

54

We Can Speak Out for God with Confidence

"Today is a scary day," my patient said as I seated her in my dental chair and draped a napkin around her neck. "And a waiting day."

"Oh, really?" I said. "Why is that?"

"My niece had brain cancer when she was ten years old and beat it. But it returned. She's in surgery right now."

"I'm so sorry," I said. "This *is* a scary waiting day. We'd better pray."

"Thank you. I knew you would."

I'm fortunate to have an employer who allows and even welcomes it when I share words of faith or moments of prayer with our patients. The spiritual breadcrumbs I sprinkle into my conversations have established me as a person of faith and provided opportunities to minister as I care for their teeth.

Yet even in such a supportive environment, sometimes I still hesitate. Especially when I wonder how a patient will respond or if they'll reject my words.

Jesus prepared His disciples for even more serious outcomes by assuring them, "When you are brought before synagogues, rulers and authorities, do not worry about how you will defend yourselves or what you will say, for the Holy Spirit will teach you at that time what you should say" (Luke 12:11–12).

God calls us to "always be prepared to give an answer to everyone who asks you to give the reason for the hope that you have" (1 Peter 3:15). Then He tells us how to give this answer: "with gentleness and respect."

God doesn't put a caveat on His command. He doesn't say, "Talk about me only with those you know are believers." Or "Share biblical truth when you know they'll agree." He says, "*Always be prepared* to give a reason for the hope you have" (emphasis added).

Discretion requires us to listen for the Holy Spirit's prompting. It calls us to respect the wishes of those we work for. But speaking up for God also requires us to take Spirit-led risks.

That day in the dental office, I knew if my beloved niece was undergoing brain surgery, I'd want someone to pray with me. We don't always have this certainty, but if the Holy Spirit prompts, we need to respond. By faith. With courage. We can trust God for the results.

> For the Holy Spirit will teach you at that time what you should say.
>
> Luke 12:12

THINK ON THIS

We can speak up for God with Spirit-led confidence.

Father, I praise You that You have given us the privilege of pointing others to You. You've entrusted to us—flawed and frail people—Your words of life, hope, and healing. Thank You for promising to give us the words to speak when we need them. When we're scared, Lord, You give us courage. Through the power of the Holy Spirit, accomplish Your mighty purposes through our simple words and Your mighty Word. Give us faith to honor You wherever we go, for others' good and Your glory. Amen.

55

We Can Point People to God

Most worshipers gazed at the screen that day as they sang along with the hymn lyrics. Others watched the vocalists as they led the music. I watched the sign language interpreter.

Dressed in black, she would have melted into the darkness of the stage if it weren't for her hands. Pale against her dark blouse, they stood out as if they'd been spotlighted.

As the music soared, they rose with it. They danced. They fluttered. They worshiped. "Then sings my soul, my Savior, God, to Thee, 'How great thou art. How great thou art!'"[13]

Out of her hands flowed words of praise and adoration. Every movement of her fingers directed our eyes to God and our hearts to worship.

If I passed this lovely lady in the foyer after the service, I doubt I'd recognize her. I suspect she prefers it this way. A modern-day John the Baptist, she understands that her calling is to point people to God, not to herself.

When John's disciples came to him, concerned that Jesus

was baptizing more people than he was, he replied, "A person can receive only what is given them from heaven. You yourselves can testify that I said, 'I am not the Messiah but am sent ahead of him.' . . . That joy is mine, and it is now complete. He must become greater; I must become less" (John 3:27–30).

We may not have the ability to preach like John or sign the lyrics of a holy hymn, but we, too, can minimize ourselves and maximize God.

Before we do anything, we can ask ourselves, Will this glorify God or glorify me? If the latter, then we must ask, What can I do differently so God gets the glory?

Can we give anonymously? Serve more humbly? Reflect the praise we receive back to God, who gave us our talents and abilities?

Can we remember our lives should be all about Him, not all about us?

He must become greater; I must become less.

John 3:30

THINK ON THIS

When we understand we were created to reflect God's magnificence, we become the velvet backdrop against which the glory of God shines.

Father, You alone deserve glory, honor, and praise. You created us to reflect Your magnificence. Guard my heart from pride and help me worship You in humility and joy. How great thou art. How great thou art!

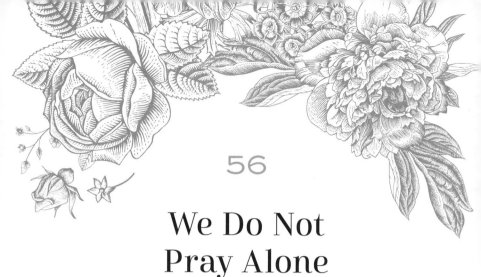

56

We Do Not Pray Alone

Have you ever faced a situation so broken you had no idea how God could mend it? This is where I found myself early one morning as I sat before the Lord.

"Oh, Father," I sighed, burying my face in my hands. "I'm scared for those I love. I want to help them, but I don't know how."

A tear escaped from my eye, and then another. And another. Before long, I was sobbing.

Scientists tell us tears release endorphins that help ease physical and emotional pain. Perhaps this is so. But it wasn't chemicals that ultimately made me feel better. What gave me the greatest comfort in the hours following my tearful prayer time was the promise of Romans 8:26. "In the same way, the Spirit helps us in our weakness. We do not know what we ought to pray for, but the Spirit himself intercedes for us through wordless groans."

I'm so grateful we don't have to figure out the answers to our prayers before we pray. God isn't waiting for us to give Him our best ideas so He can make them happen. Our most effective prayers acknowledge our impotence and trust His power. They admit our limited understanding and exalt His ultimate wisdom. When we pray this way, something incredible happens—the Spirit Himself prays with us.

"And he who searches our hearts knows the mind of the Spirit, because the Spirit intercedes for God's people in accordance with the will of God" (v. 27).

God the Holy Spirit knows the burdens of our hearts even more fully than we do. When sorrow renders us speechless or confusion silences our prayers, He speaks on our behalf with transcendent groanings. He who knows our mind and the mind of the Father bridges the gap.

I'm so grateful we do not pray alone.

> In the same way, the Spirit helps us in our weakness. We do not know what we ought to pray for, but the Spirit himself intercedes for us through wordless groans.
>
> Romans 8:26

THINK ON THIS

We do not pray alone. God the Holy Spirit prays with us.

Father, I'm so grateful You not only hear my prayers, You send Someone to help me pray. I praise You for the precious Holy Spirit, who knows my heart and Yours. When I can't even form the words, He speaks for me. I take great comfort in knowing He'll correct my prayers

when I pray anything contrary to Your will. Thank You for hearing my prayers and answering them. In the strong name of Jesus, I ask, amen.

57

He Has Risen!

I suspect Mary Magdalene and the other Mary hadn't thought through their plan (Matthew 28:1–10). Truth be told, they might not have had a plan. Under normal circumstances, when someone you loved died, you washed their body, anointed it with spices, prepared it for burial, and cried—a lot.

Crying was all they'd done, it seemed. The Sabbath had prevented them from giving Jesus a decent burial. God bless Joseph and Nicodemus. At least they'd wrapped his body and tucked it into Joseph's tomb. But then the guards sealed it up.

Their aching hearts drew them back to the tomb as soon as light dawned. They knew they had no way to pay proper homage to their Lord, but they'd tucked spices and strips of cloth in their bags, anyway.

The man who promised to be their Savior had died. When He did, hope died with Him.

But then—the earthquake. And the angel. And the glorious pronouncement—words they'd never expected to hear. "He is not here; he has risen, just as he said" (Matthew 28:6).

Not here? Risen? Before they could comprehend the words, there He was—radiant in splendor and very much alive (vv. 8–10).

"Go quickly and tell his disciples," the angel proclaimed. "'He has risen from the dead'" (v. 7).

Every Easter, churches around the world resound with the good news. "He lives! He lives! Christ Jesus lives today."

Other religious leaders died and stayed dead, but not our Savior. He conquered death and lives forever. Thomas touched Him. Peter fished with Him. Five hundred witnesses saw Him alive. The Jewish historian Josephus recorded His life, death, and resurrection. The world reset its chronology to pay tribute to Him.

Now, until He comes to judge the world and claim His bride, the church, He sits at the right hand of God—very, very much alive (Mark 16:19).

> He is not here; he has risen.
>
> Matthew 28:6

THINK ON THIS

We serve a Savior who conquered death and lives forever. He is risen!

Precious Savior, what a joy it is to know You are more powerful than death, hell, and the grave. You proved it by rising from the dead. I don't have to wonder if Your promises of eternal life are true. I can face my death and the death of my loved ones without fear, because You proved death is not the end. It's the beginning. Because You rose to eternal life, we will too. Hallelujah!

58

We Stand before God Guilt-Free

I don't remember my transgression, but in my six-year-old mind, it was bad. Maybe I talked back to my parents. Or disobeyed their instructions. Regardless, I knew I deserved to be punished. Sin squeezed my little heart like a vise. I desperately wanted to be free from the guilt and shame.

"Spank me!" I wailed. "I deserve it." (At this point in my story, my husband always shakes his head. He was the youngest of four children and needed frequent "reminders" to correct his behavior. He can't imagine anyone asking to be spanked.) But my heart was tender and needed cleansing. I knew my disobedience stood between me and my parents. I yearned for the sweetness of a guilt-free conscience.

I was eighteen years old before I learned that sin not only harms our relationships with others; it stands between us and God. The apostle Paul described it this way: "Once you were alienated from God and were enemies in your minds because of your evil behavior" (Colossians 1:21).

This sad verse, however, is followed by a very glad verse:

"But now he has reconciled you by Christ's physical body through death to present you holy in his sight, without blemish and free from accusation" (v. 22).

As I rightly deserved punishment for my childhood infractions, I also deserved punishment for the heap of sins I accumulated in the years that followed. We all did (Romans 3:23). But God sent His Son to take our punishment. Glory, hallelujah! Because of Jesus, we can stand before God holy, without blemish, and free from accusation. Imagine this. No guilt. No shame. No fear of punishment. Just unhindered fellowship with our Father God.

I still remember the gentle swat on the backside my earthly father delivered to ease my conscience and restore our fellowship. May we never forget the great punishment Jesus took on our behalf so we can enjoy guilt-free fellowship with our heavenly Father forever.

> But now he has reconciled you by Christ's physical body through death to present you holy in his sight, without blemish and free from accusation.
>
> Colossians 1:22

THINK ON THIS

Because of Jesus, we can stand before God guilt-free.

Father, thank You for sending Jesus to take away my guilt and make a way for me to enjoy a relationship

with You. He gladly took the punishment I deserved. What love! What grace. What a precious gift. I thank You that I can stand before You clean and unashamed. May my life bring You the glory and honor You deserve.

59

I'd Go Home

I settled into a hardbacked chair in the food court of the Destin–Fort Walton Beach Airport and took a sip from my four-dollar bottle of water. As a steady stream of travelers flowed past me, a young family captured my attention. A boy of eight or nine trudged wearily beside his mother. His father dragged a rolling suitcase. Draped over the carry-on like a sloth, arms dangling and eyes closed, was a little girl of about four.

As the family flopped onto the chairs beside me, mom rummaged through her backpack. She doled out goldfish crackers, raisins, and granola bars. They shared a bottle of water.

"If you could travel anywhere in the world," she said with forced enthusiasm, "where would you go?"

Like a marionette on a string, the little girl's head slowly lifted from where she'd rested it on the table. She blinked twice and said, "I'd go home."

I often feel like that little girl. I suspect Jesus's disciples felt this way, too.

On the darkest night of His earthly life, Jesus gathered His friends for one last meal. Exhausted from the strain of ministry and fearful of what the future held, they leaned in to hear His words.

"Little children," He said, "I am with you only a little while longer. . . . Where I am going, you cannot follow Me now, but you will follow later" (John 13:33, 36 BSB).

As they raised their voices in protest, He silenced them with a promise: "Do not let your hearts be troubled. You believe in God; believe in Me as well. In My Father's house are many rooms. . . . If I go and prepare a place for you, I will come back and welcome you into My presence, so that you also may be where I am" (John 14:1–3 BSB).

I don't know what home is like for you here on earth, but in heaven, home defies imagination. Filled with light, love, and laughter, its exquisite beauty will steal the breath from our lungs and the words from our mouths. We'll join the throng of angels and believers who have gone before us as they sing a chorus that echoes into eternity. "Holy, holy, holy is the Lord God Almighty" (Revelation 4:8).

And God our Father will be there.

"Well done, good and faithful servant!" He'll say as He wraps us in the hug He's been waiting our lifetime to give. "Come and share your master's happiness" (Matthew 25:23).

"Welcome home."

> If I go and prepare a place for you, I will come back and welcome you into My presence, so that you also may be where I am.
>
> John 14:3 BSB

THINK ON THIS

One day, our journey will end, and we'll be home with the Lord forever.

Father, some days, the cares of this world make me weary, and I grow homesick for heaven. Thank You for the promise of a forever life with You in a place where laughter is plentiful and joy is complete. Give me strength to serve You well for as long as I live. In Jesus's precious name I pray, amen.

60

God Engraves Us on His Hands

Early in the morning, when the sun shines just right, I can see a perfect handprint in the center of my glass kitchen door. It's been there for quite a while, but my husband just noticed it.

"There's a handprint on our door."

"Yep."

"You've seen it before?"

"Yep."

"And you left it there?"

David knows I like a neat house. Every week after my grand-kids visit for Fun Fridays at Gigi's, I pick up toys, reshelve books, and tidy up. I wipe jelly off the back of chairs and sweep popcorn off the floor.

But I left the handprint. It reminds me of my grandkids, and it makes me smile. Every time I see it, I thank God for them.

There's no chance I'll forget the four little people that bring me so much joy, but some days, a visual reminder prompts me to express my gratitude to God for them.

Perhaps this is why Jesus chose to retain the nail scars on His hands—to remind us to thank Him for His sacrificial love.

When Jesus appeared before the disciples after He rose from the dead, He extended His hands to Thomas. "Put your finger here," He said, "See my hands. . . . Stop doubting and believe" (John 20:27).

Thomas responded in faith and worship, "My Lord and my God!" (v. 28).

One day, I'll stand before Jesus. I imagine what it will be like to gaze into the eyes of Him who saw all my sin and loved me anyway. My heart will grow faint, and my knees will buckle. As Mary did at the tomb, I'll cling to His feet and cry and cry.

I'd be content to lie there forever, clinging and crying, but Jesus will raise me to my feet. He'll extend His arms, and that's when I'll see His hands—the hands that took the nails for me.

I'll remember His promise, "I have loved you with an ever-lasting love. . . . I have engraved you on the palms of my hands" (Jeremiah 31:3; Isaiah 49:16).

My tears will flow again as gratitude overwhelms my soul.

"Thank You," I'll whisper as He envelopes me in a heavenly hug. "Thank You so much."

> See, I have engraved you on the palms of my hands.
>
> Isaiah 49:16

THINK ON THIS

The handprints of Jesus serve as a permanent reminder of how much He loves us.

Precious Jesus, I don't deserve the sacrifice You made for me on the cross. I was Your enemy, yet You loved me anyway. You allowed sinful men to beat You. They spat on You, yanked out Your beard, and pierced Your scalp with thorns. And then they nailed You to a cross. You suffered an agonizing death—for me and for all mankind. Thank You. Thank You. Thank You.

How to Have a Relationship with God

The Bible tells us how we can have a relationship with God: We must understand that we have sinned, and our sin offends a holy God.

> For all have sinned and fall short of the glory of God. (Romans 3:23)

Because we are sinners, we're separated from God, and deserve to die and spend eternity in hell.

> For the wages of sin is death. (Romans 6:23)

We can't do anything to earn our place in heaven.

> For it is by grace you have been saved, through faith—and this is not from yourselves, it is the gift of God—not by works, so that no one can boast. (Ephesians 2:8–9)

God loved us so much that He sacrificed His sinless, perfect Son Jesus, to pay for our sin.

> For God so loved the world that he gave his one and only Son, that whoever believes in him shall not perish but have eternal life. (John 3:16)

> God made him who had no sin to be sin for us, so that in him we might become the righteousness of God. (2 Corinthians 5:21)

We must be willing to repent (turn away from) our sin and accept by faith what Jesus did for us on the cross.

When we do this, God promises us a relationship with Him, forgiveness from our sin, and a forever home in heaven.

> But the gift of God is eternal life in Christ Jesus our Lord. (Romans 6:23)

If you want to have a relationship with God, tell Him.

Here's a sample prayer:

God, I know that I am a sinner who doesn't deserve a place in Your heaven. Today I repent of my sin, and I surrender my life to You. I accept what Jesus did for me when He died on the cross. Come into my heart, God, and make me a new person.

If you prayed this prayer, or said the same thing in your own words, and really meant it, God has something to say to you:

> If you declare with your mouth, "Jesus is Lord,"
> and believe in your heart that God raised him
> from the dead, you will be saved. (Romans 10:9)

If you decided to follow Christ, I want to rejoice with you and help you on your way. Please visit me on my website (LoriHatcher.com) and drop me a note.

Finally, I encourage you to read the Bible, beginning with the book of John. Find a Bible-believing church in your area so you can grow in your new spiritual life and get to know God's family, the church.

Again, congratulations. You've just made the most important decision of your life. Welcome to the family of God!

Notes

1. "Answers," Billy Graham Evangelistic Association, last modified May 6, 2021, https://billygraham.org/answer /three-kinds-of-peace-what-the-bible-says/.
2. A. Brennan, et al., "The South Carolina Floods of October 2015," Carolinas Integrated Sciences & Assessments (CISA), accessed May 10, 2024, https://cisa.sc.edu/PDFs /October%202015%20Flood%20Event%204%20Pager.pdf.
3. Deena Bouknight, "Flooded with Hope," *Reach Out Columbia*, October 2016.
4. "450 Turkish Sheep Leap to Their Deaths," Fox News, last modified January 13, 2015, https://www.foxnews.com /story/450-turkish-sheep-leap-to-their-deaths.
5. To read more about Linda's story, visit her website, www .authorlindasummerford.com.
6. John Newton, "Amazing Grace! (how sweet the sound)," Hymnary.org, accessed April 2, 2023, https://hymnary.org /text/amazing_grace_how_sweet_the_sound.
7. Julia H. Johnston, "Grace Greater than Our Sin," Hymnary .org, accessed April 2, 2023, https://hymnary.org/text /marvelous_grace_of_our_loving_lord.
8. Joni Eareckson Tada, *A Step Further* (Grand Rapids, MI: Zondervan, 1980), 47.

9. Grayson Weir, "Tom Brady's Unique Statistical Record As A Receiver Is Something Every Sports Fan Needs To Know," BroBible, last modified February 3, 2022, https://brobible.com/sports/article/tom-brady-receiving-yards-over-40/.
10. Weir, "Tom Brady's Unique Statistical Record."
11. Brandon D. Smith, "Why Augustine Centered His Life on the Trinity and Why We Should Care," Desiring God, accessed May 15, 2024, https://www.desiringgod.org/articles/why-augustine-centered-his-life-on-the-trinity.
12. A. W. Tozer, *Of God and Men* (Chicago: Moody, 2015), 77.
13. Carl Gustav Boberg, "How Great Thou Art," Hymnary.org, accessed May 14, 2024, https://hymnary.org/text/o_lord_my_god_when_i_in_awesome_wonder.

About the Author

In the spirit of Philippians 4:8, Lori chose sixty-six words, one for each book of the Bible, to describe the true, noble, right, pure, lovely, admirable, excellent, or praiseworthy parts of her life:

God, her family, the Bible and the church, reading, writing, and maple walnut ice cream.

Reese's peanut butter cups, sunshine, honesty, integrity, Christian brothers and sisters.

Edisto Island, long prayer walks, hot showers, warm puppies, and cold watermelon.

Quiet lunches with friends; Bristol, Rhode Island; and the North Carolina mountains.

Teaching at Christian writers conferences, taking cruises, laughing, and eating food she doesn't have to cook.

Lori would love to continue the conversation. Subscribe to her blog, *Refresh* (LoriHatcher.com), to receive weekly email encouragement.

Did *Think on These Things* bless you? Share your thoughts in a review on Amazon, Goodreads, or wherever you shop for books. Thoughtful reviews help other readers find great resources.

Spread the Word
by Doing One Thing.

- Give a copy of this book as a gift.
- Share the QR code link via your social media.
- Write a review of this book on your blog, favorite bookseller's website, or at ODB.org/store.
- Recommend this book to your church, small group, or book club.

Connect with us. 🇫 🄾

Our Daily Bread Publishing
PO Box 3566, Grand Rapids, MI 49501, USA
Email: books@odb.org

Love God. Love Others.

with  **Our Daily Bread.**

Your gift changes lives.

Connect with us. 🅵 🅾

Our Daily Bread Publishing
PO Box 3566, Grand Rapids, MI 49501, USA
Email: books@odb.org